No Experience Necessary

Contacting and Inviting
Made Easy

NO EXPERIENCE NECESSARY

CONTACTING AND INVITING...
MADE EASY

RON BAKER

DreamHouse
Publishing

www.dreamhousepublishing.com

DreamHouse

2100 Blossom Way South
St. Petersburg, Fl 33712

Copyright © 2004 by Ronald G. Baker Jr.

ISBN 1-9325830-6-8

Printed in the United States of America.

Special discounts on bulk quantities are available from DreamHouse Publishing.
Contact dreamhouseorders@hgml.net

Cover design by Zrahid Croy.

Contents

**"I will study
and prepare and
one day my chance
will come."**

—ABRAHAM LINCOLN

Introduction

Never before has there been a greater need for us to take control of our financial destiny. People of all ages are turning to entrepreneurship to regain power over their financial futures, so that security and success are held in their control.

Picture the man or woman who drive their dream car, live in a great house, have several vacation homes, give generously and regularly to worthy charities, have financial security, and are recognized and admired for their accomplishments. Chances are very good that these people: 1) are in business for themselves; and, 2) started their business exactly where you are today - sitting with an empty calendar, a list of prospects, and staring at the phone.

Their success secret (if there is a secret) is that they first had to learn new ways of thinking as well as new skills. Then they applied these new attitudes and skills over and over until wealth-building habits developed. These habits are what it takes to move any business forward. One of these habits is the skill of <u>getting a product, service and/or opportunity in front of as many qualified prospects as possible.</u>

Developing the confidence, skill and discipline of consistently and effectively setting appointments is vital to your success. This book focuses on the essential development of momentum-building, appointment-setting habits. The following pages provide a step-by-step plan for developing the skills necessary to set as many appointments as you desire. This proven system will work for anyone who follows the program.

Have you ever said to yourself, "how can *Contacting and Inviting* {*be*} *Made Easy* for me?" Well you're not alone. Over the past two decades I have met, coached, and worked with countless business professionals in every industry imaginable. Some were just getting started while others were seasoned veterans. But all struggled daily with that same question.

The term "Contacting and Inviting" as it relates to this book, is simply the process of initiating contact with someone you may or may not know. Then your goal is to set an appointment with those who are <u>open</u> to exploring the value of your product, service, opportunity or offering. That's it! It is no more complicated than that. The purpose of this book is to provide a template or system that, when applied, will generate a calendar filled with productive business building appointments.

An appointment can take on several different forms. For example, an appointment can be a face-to-face meeting with a single prospect, a conference call, a group meeting, a seminar or workshop, an open house, or even a webcast. The good news is that the principles used to first make contact, and then to convince a prospect to invest a bit of time, are the same for any setting. This means that anyone, and I mean anyone, who takes the time to follow the principles presented in the following pages, can develop the ability to not only fill their own calendar with appointments, but to teach and pass on these valuable skills to others.

Over the past 20 years I have been making contact with and inviting prospects to explore the value of doing business with my company and me. In addition, I have taught thousands of people from various industries time-tested principles and techniques on how to comfortably and confidently contact prospective clients and invite them to explore a business relationship. In the following pages you will discover these time-tested principles and techniques that work just as effectively for someone selling computer systems integration for a Fortune 100 company as they do for those pursuing their financial freedom in the explosive home-based business industry. The process is the same regardless of the individual, industry, product or service. You may be thinking, *"Sure, these principles and techniques may work for some people. But my situation, products, opportunity, business, personality, company, and competition is different. What makes you think your methods will work for me?"*

Good question. I (humbly) have an equally good answer. The reason the principles and techniques in *Contacting and Inviting Made Easy* will work for everyone (including you) is because you, and those with whom you make contact, are living, breathing people. And one thing I have learned over the past 20 years is that people in general are very predictable. Individuals who make their living by initiating contact with prospects every day are just as predictable as those being contacted. *Contacting and Inviting Made Easy* takes the guesswork out of this often very challenging, yet very lucrative skill set. Read on and learn how to make contacting and inviting easy for both you and your prospects.

Humble Beginnings

I began my career selling office equipment for a Fortune 100 company in the early 1980s, and have been involved in sales or sales training ever since. However, my career was nearly cut short by a single disastrous event.

The very first day in the office, Gerry, my manager, told me that I knew everything there was to know about our products and the competition, and that it was time to share this knowledge with prospective customers. *"Are you ready to call on prospects?"* he asked. *"Yes, sir,"* I replied. So out the door I enthusiastically went, brochures and price list in hand.

Entering the first office building, I walked up to the receptionist full of confidence, expecting to be welcomed with open arms. I remember it like it was yesterday. I said something like this: *"Who buys office equipment for your company?"* What happened next nearly ended my career on the spot. In front of a lobby full of people and in a very loud condescending voice, the receptionist said, *"I don't know who you are, or what you think you are doing, but we do not need or want what you are selling. Leave now and don't come back without an appointment."* I felt the eyes of everyone in the lobby on me as I made for the door. Almost in tears, I returned to the safety of my office. I remember telling my manager that I didn't think I was cut out for sales and that I was sorry I had wasted his time.

Gerry smiled and said, *"Rather than quitting before lunch on your first Monday, let me coach you on a much better way to get in front of your prospects. If you are willing to follow a few simple steps, I'm sure you'll make it."*

Then he asked me the question of a lifetime, *"Are you coachable?"*

I am embarrassed to admit it, but I had to think about his offer. I had just experienced the most humiliating, embarrassing form of rejection. I was paralyzed with fear and self-doubt.

"You're sure I can make it?" I asked. *"Absolutely!"* Gerry said. *"I guarantee it, but only if you follow my instructions to the letter."*

Gerry explained that being coachable meant taking on faith that what he told me to do <u>would</u> work, even if it felt a bit uncomfortable at first. *"Just give it the day. Fair enough?"* he asked. I agreed. My experience the very next day put me on the road to success.

During that life-changing day, I learned the power and efficiency of setting appointments by using the phone. The phone became my most valuable business partner. The better we (my phone and I) worked together, the more money I made.

Setting appointments over the phone gave me time to build rapport and interest so that my prospects actually looked forward to our meeting. I could make more money in less time by meeting face-to-face with the right people who had an interest in seeing me and learning about my products. I was able to meet with prospects who were motivated to explore options and who held the authority to make decisions.

I learned to create Momentum in record time and with laser focus. I define Momentum as that professional state where your career is on a positive roll, your calendar is full of appointments with qualified prospects. You look forward to the next day. Business is good and your attitude is strong. A business with momentum is hard to stop. The more appointments I set, the more confident I felt and the more success I had.

In the following months, I went to bed each night knowing my calendar was full. I looked forward to what the next day would bring. My belief and professional self-image were bulletproof.

The appointment-setting process I perfected and taught over the past 20 years is yours in the following pages. Whether you are the owner of a sub shop calling local businesses to promote your new lunchtime catering service; a direct salesperson selling multi-million-dollar computer systems; or the owner of a home-based business calling prospects in the evening; the principles and techniques you are about to discover not only work, but they work well. I am confident that if you follow this program to the letter, you can learn everything required to fill your calendar with appointments.

The chapters in this book discuss specific issues relating to the contacting and inviting process. Each chapter introduces a new concept, builds on what you have learned in the previous chapter and may contain a brief exercise. It is important that you follow the book exactly as it is laid out, completing each exercise in order.

Do this, and I am confident that you will not only see your skills grow right before your eyes, but you will also be able to pass this knowledge on to others. The experience of helping others to achieve a greater level of skill, confidence and success can be as rewarding as your own personal achievements. I hope you find this book a valued partner in this journey.

"Twenty years from now you will be more disappointed by the things you didn't do than by the ones you did do. So throw off the bowlines. Sail away from the safe harbour. Catch the trade winds in your sails. Explore. Dream. Discover."

—MARK TWAIN

Chapter One

What's Holding You Back?

I have heard people say, *"I know my prospects would be as excited as I am if they only knew how great this product, service or business is."* Nothing could be truer. Your excitement and commitment can be infectious when your prospects are given the opportunity to see your belief and enthusiasm. But, for them to see it, you need to set the appointment. Other than just plain old-fashioned laziness, there are only two reasons for a general lack of appointments:

- The <u>fear and hesitation</u> of using the phone to make business contacts — what I describe as <u>Contact Hesitation.</u>
- The lack of appointment-setting skills — knowing what to say and how to say it.

Some people are just afraid to pick up the phone to make prospecting calls. These people either never get going at all or only make a few calls; they never generate enough positive activity to succeed.

On the other end of the spectrum, there are the fearless ones who can burn through a prospect list in no time. However, they lack basic skills. In the absence of these skills, they can turn a great prospect list into a worthless pile of paper and end up discouraged and defeated.

Does this sound like anyone you know? You, perhaps?

Fear no longer — the following principles and techniques are not based on theory; they are time-and field-tested. The results are predictable and the formula is simple. Read, apply and discover the possibilities.

Fear Revealed

Public television recently aired a documentary on the Indian Bengal tiger. Most impressive was the strength, grace and confidence the tiger projected as it mastered its domain. This documentary detailed how these magnificent animals are hunted for sport. Before the hunt begins, a clearing is prepared by unrolling a 5-foot-tall strip of cheesecloth around the perimeter, leaving one side open for the tiger to enter.

There, a group of men with high-powered rifles ride atop several elephants. They enter the forest where a tiger is believed to be sleeping. Running alongside the elephants are several other men with drums and sticks. Their goal is to make enough noise so as to scare the tiger out of its home and toward the clearing, where more hunters await.

Once the tiger enters the clearing, two men hiding in the trees stretch more cheesecloth across the opening, trapping the tiger inside a cheesecloth cage.

To the tiger, the cheesecloth might as well be a 30-foot-tall brick wall. The hunters celebrate as the tiger experiences paralyzing fear, running around the perimeter looking for an opening. As the frantic tiger looks for a way out, a single bullet ends the hunt.

We all know the tiger could have escaped with little or no difficulty. It could have easily ripped through the cheesecloth or simply jumped over it. In fact, the tiger was never physically trapped at all.

The tiger was trapped only by its <u>perception</u> that the cheesecloth was an inescapable barrier, not by the barrier itself. This is an important point. The false perception or mindset killed the action required for the tiger to regain its freedom, return to the familiar view of the forest and save its own life. Fear gave the cheesecloth the power to hold, control, and enslave the tiger.

Similar to the tiger in the story, we can be trapped by our own cheesecloth cages. A negative perception can distort truth, giving life and power to fear. Fear, no matter its cause, can prevent action. Lack of action (or lack of prospecting) will most definitely limit the exposure of your business, products, ideas and/or services to others. This will limit your success. One does not need a Ph.D. in psychology to understand the stranglehold that Contact Hesitation can have on productivity.

The first step to successfully setting appointments is to change your perceptions that give the life and power to your fear. Our objective is to remove this fear so that it no longer can hold your actions hostage. In fact, this new insight will actually fuel positive thoughts, so that rather than being held hostage by fear, you will find it difficult to hold back your enthusiasm as you reach for the phone.

I have heard people say, <u>action cures fear</u>. You know it as the *"just-pick-up-the-phone-and-do-it"* mentality. Perhaps it is true for some that action alone will win over fear. But what happens to the person who is too afraid to act? If fear is preventing them from getting started, what then?

If my manager had given me this *"just-do-it"* counsel when I returned from my first disastrous attempt in the field, I would have never had the fortunes of my success. Without a doubt, I would have been too hesitant to act. My performance would have suffered and I would have sought, or been forced to seek, a different line of work.

Skills, Skills, Skills

I remember hearing a story about a lumberjack who walked into a camp looking for work. To prove he was the best lumberjack the foreman had ever seen, he boasted that he could chop down more trees than anyone in the history of the company. Given the chance to prove himself, the lumberjack set out for the woods bright and early with the goal of chopping down 10 trees that day. As the story goes, he only felled nine trees the first day, tying the previously established record. With stern determination he set out to beat the record on the second day, only to fell seven trees. On day three, putting in just as many hours, his production fell again, with only five trees hitting the ground.

"I have never worked so hard and gotten so little done," the lumberjack thought to himself. *"I don't understand it."* On the fourth day, he set out for the woods an hour earlier than the three days before. The foreman stopped him just as he left camp. "I notice you are working pretty hard and getting less and less done. What do you think is wrong?" he asked. *"I don't know,"* said the lumberjack. *"I have never worked so hard and not hit my goals. I guess I just need to work harder."*

With a big smile, the foreman said, *"I know you've been busy, but in the past few days, have you taken the time to sharpen your axe?"*

Well, you guessed it — the lumberjack had not sharpened his axe since he set out to break the record. In fact, he came to camp with a dull axe. Without knowing it, the odds were stacked against him. The dull axe he held in his hands limited his production and kept him from his goal. It is also important to note that the harder he worked without reaching his goal, the more frustrated and discouraged he became.

Let's apply this story to the proper, productive way to use the phone to set appointments. It's likely you have used the phone at least once during every day you can remember.

Without realizing it, over the years you have developed some basic phone skills. However, using the phone to set business appointments is quite different and requires new skills. Going forward without taking the time to first learn these skills, and then master them, is just like our lumberjack friend setting out to do his job carrying an unsharpened axe.

Would you rather work with a sharp axe, make progress and be excited with the results? Or would you like to work really hard with a dull axe, make little progress and become discouraged? It doesn't sound like a difficult question, but picking up the phone to set appointments without first sharpening the <u>right skills</u> is much like trying to set the all-time tree felling record by using a dull axe.

This is why one person can invest an hour on the phone and set enough appointments for the entire week, becoming enthused and excited about the week ahead. Then others can spend that same hour working with undeveloped skills, get nowhere and become discouraged. These people feel as if they are spinning their wheels. They begin to doubt their business, their product and their abilities, and never reach their full potential.

Defeating the fear of the phone and sharpening new appointment-setting skills are all that stand between you and achieving your dreams.

"Progress is the activity of today and the assurance of tomorrow."

—Ralph Waldo Emerson

Chapter Two

Defeat Contact Hesitation
Once and for All

In this chapter we will take a closer look at the thoughts that give life to the fears keeping so many from properly and effectively using the phone as a prospecting tool.

Remembering how the tiger was trapped by its perception that the flimsy cheesecloth couldn't be broken, we can imagine what would have happened if that same group of hunters found themselves eye to eye with a tiger that knew the cage was only cheesecloth.

What if the tiger knew that this was an attempt on its life, its freedom and its family? Imagine for a moment that the same tiger that entered the clearing and saw the white cheesecloth heard a voice from the other side, a familiar voice of another tiger saying, *"Hey, don't be afraid; it's only cheesecloth. You can run right through it. These yo-yos tried this on me just last week. Come on — you can make it!"*

Imagine what would happen if at that critical moment, the weakness of the cheesecloth was revealed to the trapped tiger. Picture the change in the tiger's posture — a move from fear to anger, a newfound attitude of strength and confidence that only moments ago reflected fright and confusion.

Imagine the look in the tiger's eye as it realizes there is nothing to be afraid of. Free from the false perception that held it hostage, the tiger is now empowered to act, and breaks through to freedom, never to be trapped again!

Contact Hesitation Is Normal

Dealing with a new situation can be uncomfortable for anyone. Calling for appointments may be a new experience for you, so relax — it's normal to feel those butterflies. Most everyone who has used the phone to set appointments, regardless of skill level, has experienced Contact Hesitation. For some it's just an annoyance. For others, this uneasy feeling of hesitation turns into paralyzing fear.

The fears that result in Contact Hesitation are fueled by our thoughts and perceptions. It is how we think that creates fear and limits our success. The bad news is that many of us have thought this way for most of our professional lives.

The good news is that we can control and change how we think for the better. We can choose to think differently, think positively and think correctly! In developing a new way of thinking, we can develop an understanding that there is really nothing to be afraid of. In fact, there is a lot to be excited about, look forward to and enthusiastically share with others.

Let me first say that I am not a psychologist. I speak from the point of view of a sales professional who has experienced these fears firsthand and has spent years studying why setting appointments is such a difficult skill for so many to master.

I believe it boils down to this: most, if not all fears relating to Contact Hesitation are rooted in the negative anticipation of *"What will they think?"*

We all care at some level about how others perceive us. We are especially concerned with how we are perceived by those we love, respect or believe have a higher status in life. We choose to believe whether we are perceived positively or negatively by others.

Those with a negative anticipation of *"What will they think?"* believe that the people upon whom they call don't want to be bothered, don't need what they are offering, and think that the caller is only interested in getting their money.

People with a <u>positive</u> anticipation of *"What will they think?"* believe that their prospects will be glad that they called, need what they have to offer, and believe the caller is looking out for their well being.

I remember going through some old files a former sales rep had left before moving on to another assignment. One file was labeled in big bold red letters, <u>*"The Rudest Man I have ever dealt with. Don't bother."*</u>

By this time, my sales career was on a roll and I was not afraid to call anyone. Looking through the file, it appeared that the prospect had evaluated our products about a year ago and decided to stay with a competitor's equipment. Looking further into the file, I learned that he was the decision-maker for not one, not two, but six pieces of production equipment which represented almost half my semi-annual quota.

Knowing the competition as I did, I recognized that he couldn't be that happy with his current situation, so I picked up a script I had developed for these types of calls and dialed his direct line. Fully expecting him to be as rude to me as he had been to the last guy, I listened to the ringing phone, thinking to myself, *"This should be interesting"*. The conversation went something like this:

Ron: *"John Smith? Ron Baker from Eastman Kodak's Copy Products Division. We have not met yet, but I believe you spent some time with Jim Matthews evaluating our duplicating equipment. Did I reach you at a bad time?"*

Mr. Smith: *"What did you say your name was?"*

Ron: *"Ron Baker with —"*

Mr. Smith: (cutting me off — you see, he really <u>was</u> rude) *"Yes-yes, with Eastman Kodak's Copy Products. I know, I know — actually, this is not a bad time."*

Ron: *"Great — the reason why I'm calling is to ask for a bit of your time to introduce myself and acquaint you with some of our new products. What days this week are you tied — "* (I couldn't believe it; he cut me off again!)

Mr. Smith: *"Stop by tomorrow at 10:00."*

Ron: *"Terrific — 10:00 at your office on University Ave."*

Mr. Smith: *"No, I have moved my office to Union Square; 22 Union Square, fifth floor."*

Ron: *"Glad I confirmed — I am writing in my calendar 10:00 tomorrow at your office on the fifth floor of 22 Union Square —"* (click — he hung up on me. He really was the rudest man I had ever met. He never even said goodbye.)

As it turned out, Mr. Smith needed what I had to offer. He was glad that I called and over the next several years became one of my best customers. In fact, he even offered himself as a reference, gladly recommending my products (in his own rude way) to anyone who asked.

This all took place because I chose to have a positive anticipation of *"What will they think?"*. I knew if he had our products, he would be happy. I knew he would be better off dealing with me rather than the competition. I knew it and believed it, and because I was so sure, I was not afraid to call him on the phone to set up some time to meet with him and share what I knew about my products. I took action and won.

You might be thinking, *"Yes, but what if this Mr. Smith guy didn't want to see you? What if he was not interested? What if you took action and did not win this time? What then?"*

I can answer that with one single word: Next! I would have just saved myself some time. I still believe I have the best product and service to offer. If Mr. Smith, or anyone else, is not ready to hear about it now, that does not change the fact that I believe what I offer is of value. Protect your attitude by professionally ending the call quickly and moving on.

Turn Hesitation Into Enthusiasm
Answer this question quickly without thinking about it. Would you call your neighbor at 3:30 in the morning? No? Why not? Is it because they might not want to be bothered? Perhaps they might think poorly of you? OK, how about this: What if your neighbor's house was on fire? Do you think your neighbor would mind a call from you then? Do you think your neighbor would consider your call an intrusion of privacy? A bother? Perhaps they might be glad you called?

This example may be a bit extreme, but the point is the same. If you believe you have a compelling reason to call, then you will not hesitate! Calling someone is not a big deal as long as you have something important to discuss and something of value to offer.

For me it was easy. I had compelling reasons why someone

would want to meet with me. These compelling reasons were clear in my mind, and I believed them. In short, my perception was, *"Who wouldn't want to hear about Kodak's great equipment?"* I believed without a doubt that a prospect who needed my type of equipment would value their benefits, but would only be able to enjoy them after they knew about them. And it was up to me to tell them.

What are your reasons to call your prospects? Do you know them by heart? What is it about your offerings that will bring happiness or somehow enhance your prospect's personal or professional life? And here's the real question: <u>Do you</u> <u>believe it?</u> Believing that you are calling with something that can make others happy, or in some way enhance their lives, gives you the <u>power of positive antic-ipation.</u> Your mind switches from *"I might be bothering them"* to *"I bet they will be glad I called."*

Take a moment and think of the top three benefits your prospect stands to enjoy should they decide to see you. Write them in the spaces provided below. If you can list more than three, that's terrific, but you need to have at least three. We will use these benefits later on as we build custom dialogue.

1. _____
2. _____
3. _____
4.

Now, don't keep it a SECRET!

There is a lot of psychobabble published by some really smart people who in 400-plus pages can tell you in detail about every prospecting related fear you could imagine: fear of failure; fear of rejection; fear of self-promotion; and on and on. Of all I have experienced and read on the subject, I have found nothing that does not sound any more complex than the negative anticipation of *"What will they think?".* So from this point on, I won't bore you with any other reasons for you or anyone else to be afraid to pick up the phone. Trust me — it is no more complicated that this.

Believe that your prospects:

- will be glad you called.
- need what you have to offer.
- know you are looking out for their well-being.

Do this and you will have this fear licked.

If you are anything like me, you occasionally hear those voices in your mind telling you that you *"can't do it,"* or are unworthy of success, or what you have to offer may not be worth the trouble. If this is true for you, I will share with you a valuable truth: <u>The voices lie. They are the voices of dream stealers, hope robbers and success thieves</u>. I have been in their company, and I have discovered that when I hold them up to the value I offer and the dreams I chase, they melt away. Just as the cheesecloth cage that trapped the tiger would have instantly become powerless with a simple change of thought and perception, a simple yet powerful change in our thought processes can tear down the barriers that keep us from reaching our full potential.

However, these thoughts rarely change on their own or without some work. We need to feed our minds with thoughts and ideas that reinforce the truth about our potential, self-worth and ability to succeed. I encourage you to feed your mind with positive input just as you would feed your body with nourishing food. This healthy <u>mind food</u> comes in many forms: tapes, audio CDs, books, and associations with individuals who uplift and challenge you in ways that guide you to your goals and dreams. I encourage you to be generous to yourself and indulge yourself with this positive mind food. This is one area in life where I have found that too much of a good thing is never enough. Remember, it is you against the cheesecloth. My bet is on you!

"Opportunity is missed by most people because it is dressed in overalls and looks like work."

— THOMAS EDISON

Chapter Three

Sharpen Your Skills
with STEER™

A sharp axe would have saved our lumberjack friend a great deal of time and helped him reach his goal. The same can be said of our telephone skills. Effective phone-prospecting skills can be one of your most valuable assets as you promote your business. You want your prospect to hear a knowledgeable, confident voice with something valuable to share.

Picking up the phone and <u>winging it</u>, or just using one script for every prospect type, is a waste of time and opportunity. This is unfair to you and your prospect. You don't want to sound like you are reading someone else's words from a piece of paper. Your prospects are valuable. For your sake and theirs, take a few moments to ensure that your invitation is delivered powerfully and confidently.

Experience has shown that the best results come as a result of:

A. Customizing dialogue to a specific prospect and meeting type.
B. Knowing the compelling reasons why a prospect would be motivated to see you.
C. Having strategies to manage a prospect's resistance to an appointment is what I refer to as <u>Appointment Pushback.</u>

For example, a custom script inviting a current customer to a seminar or an open house is much different than one to set a one-to-one appointment with a new prospect. All the dialogue should be focused towards gaining a commitment of time for either a one-to-one meeting or a group presentation. Each script should have important differences designed for each prospect type and meeting venue.

Tailored scripts get the best results. The following process has been developed over the years to customize scripts for maximum effectiveness with each prospect type. Without question, taking a few moments to customize scripts saves time and generates more money.

There are three basic prospect types.

1. <u>Current Customers</u>: those with whom your company currently maintains a relationship. They know you and your company, and are happy with the relationship.

2. <u>Former Customer or Engaged Prospects</u>: someone who either had your company's products at one time or had considered your company's products. These are prospects with some knowledge of your company and its products.

3. <u>Referrals:</u> Good friends or business associates of your current happy customers to whom you had not yet been introduced.

Prospect types in Relationship Marketing are surprisingly similar to those prospect types found in Corporate America:

1. <u>Good Friends:</u> As with a Current Customer, they know you well and are comfortable with the relationship.

2. <u>Acquaintances:</u> Similar to a Former Customer or Engaged Prospect, these are people with some level of contact with you.

3. <u>Referrals:</u> These are prospects passed on to you by either a Good Friend or an Acquaintance.

Putting together a custom script for each prospect type will save you time and aggravation, and most definitely increase your productivity. You may already be using a script to set appointments. If you are getting good results with your current scripts, that's great. Read on and learn what makes a good script even more effective.

An effective script has *five* specific elements. Over the years I have developed STEER™, a script-enhancing process that ensures that each element is addressed, understood and acted upon with confidence.

These five essential elements are:
1. **S**et the prospect at ease.
2. **T**ake control and guide the conversation.
3. **E**nthusiastically assume the appointment.
4. **E**xpect then manage Appointment Pushback.
5. **R**eaffirm after confirming the appointment date, time and location.

Each essential element, when used in order, creates a script that sounds natural, filters out unqualified prospects and generates results. In addition to the five STEER™ elements, there is a floating technique called Clear the Availability. This technique floats because it is the only technique that can be part of either Element No. 2 or No. 3.

Simply put, Clear the Availability means you help your prospect find time to meet with you. This technique is effective for all prospect types and is mostly used at the end of Element No. 3. However, an exception is made when calling a good friend. Let's look in closer detail at each of these five elements and how our floating technique can be applied.

**If we all did things
we were capable of,
we would astound
ourselves."**

— THOMAS EDISON

Chapter Four

STEER™ Element No. 1:
Set the Prospect at Ease

Picking up a ringing phone, whether at the office or at home, can be risky. We often don't know who is calling and we don't want to be bothered. Perhaps the caller wants to sell us something, or ask that we donate to a cause. This can create a sense of defensiveness in your prospects even before they answer the phone. For your prospects to be open to your message, it is essential that they first be <u>set at ease.</u>

The best way to set any prospect at ease is with a <u>statement of familiarity</u>. Such a statement must be made early in the call to capture attention, create interest and raise the level of comfort your prospect has with the call. Let's look at how you might set your different prospect types at ease.

Good Friends

When calling good friends, they will be set at ease because they recognize the sound of your voice and/or your name. A friend is accustomed to receiving calls from you and will not assume a defensive posture. It is important that you retain the same greeting, introduction and tone of voice your friends are used to hearing from you, thus setting them at ease. For example, if I am calling my lifelong friend Frank, I would say something like this:

Ron: *"Hey Frank, it's Ron."*

Even though Frank recognizes my voice, I make it a habit of saying my name anyway. By stating my name in the greeting, I avoid any chance that Frank will not immediately recognize me. In this case, our conversation begins just like the hundreds of others we have had. My tone is the same, and he is generally glad that I called.

The next time you call a good friend for any reason, take note of what you naturally say. Do you state your name as an introduction, or not? You most likely have not paid much attention to this over the years, but now it is important to be aware of what your friends are used to hearing when you call so that you can be consistent. For example, imagine if my call to my good friend Frank went something like this:

Ron: *"Frank Smith, this is Ron Baker calling. How are you today? I am representing ABC company..."*

Knowing Frank the way I do, he would think I had lost my mind. Once he knew I was not joking around and wanted to discuss business with him, he would immediately know that I am unsure and uncomfortable. If any prospect thinks the caller is unsure or uncomfortable, you can bet the defenses will go up and the call will go downhill from there.

Acquaintances:

To set acquaintances at ease, state immediately in the call the common thread you share. Does the prospect know you from a sporting event, or did you attend the same wedding recently? Did you go to high school together but have not spoken in 10 or more years? In some cases, you may need to re-introduce yourself. Here's an example:

Ron: *"Hi Don, this is Ron Baker. We met at Sally and Rick's wedding last week."*

Don: *"Hello, how are you doing?"*

Later in Chapter Ten you will be asked to organize your prospect list and write down how a prospect will remember you. This information will be critical when calling an acquaintance.

In the example above, the common thread (Sally and Rick's wedding) and my name are stated in the first sentence. When calling an acquaintance, set the prospect at ease by associating your name with a recent, positive and/or familiar encounter or event. You must make sure your statement of familiarity is strong, unlike the following:

Ron: *"Hi Don, this is Ron Baker. Remember me?"*

Don: *"No. Should I?"*

Assuming your prospect will remember you can be dangerous, as well as a blow to your ego. The truth is that you may not make a memorable impression on everyone with whom you come in contact. (Don't feel bad; few people do.) If your prospect doesn't remember you, it may be embarrassing, or worse yet, the prospect may confuse you with someone else. Either way, it's not a good idea to start a call with a quiz. Play it safe with a strong statement of familiarity.

Referral:

When calling on referrals, it is important that you first <u>warm</u> the prospects by letting them know that you came to have their name through a positive association you both share — <u>not</u> a cold prospect list. It is important that you first state the positive association existing between you and your prospect, immediately followed by your name. The association is stated early in your dialogue to set the prospect at ease.

Example:

Ron: *"Don, we haven't been introduced yet, but we have a common friend in Bob Hall. My name is Ron Baker."*

Saying Bob Hall's name up front <u>before</u> I introduce myself gives me the leverage of Don's familiarity with his friend Rob. The comfort Don has with Rob Hall is immediately transferred to me. Now Don is open to listening, and may in fact be interested in the purpose of the call.

"I am certainly not one who needs to be prodded. In fact, if anything, I am the prod.

— Sir Winston Churchill

Chapter Five

STEER™ Element No. 2: Take Control

Prospecting calls are made with one purpose in mind: <u>to gain a commitment for an appointment.</u> In order to accomplish this, your mission is to control the content and flow of the call, set the proper expectation, and maintain the prospect's attention.

Good Friend:

Calling a good friend with the intent to discuss business requires that you <u>do not</u> allow yourself to fall into meaningless or idle chitchat. Once the call takes this direction, it is nearly impossible to move the conversation back to business. <u>Take control</u> of the conversation by making a statement differentiating this telephone conversation from others you have had with this friend. Stating <u>up front</u> that you only have a couple of seconds tells the prospect that this call will be brief and is important. Because you are calling a good friend, you can also take the opportunity to guide him or her to <u>clear their availability</u> early in the dialogue. Unlike calls to an acquaintance or referral, clearing the availability of a good friend can be done tactfully and still sound natural.

Example:

Ron: *"Hey Frank, I only have a couple of seconds. Listen, what are you doing next Tuesday after 7:00 besides watching TV?"*

Notice that, in this example I took control of the call <u>and</u> checked Frank's availability. Because Frank and I are long-time friends, he will not find my question about Tuesday night to be pushy or out of the ordinary. I would not have this latitude with an acquaintance or referral at this point; hence the need for custom scripts.

If Frank's answer to the question is something like *"Nothing. Why?"*, a couple of things have happened. First, He just told me he has nothing of great importance going on and thus is available for a meeting. Second, by asking why, Frank is expressing interest in why I am inquiring. However, if Frank's answer sounds something like:

Frank: *"Tuesday at 7:00 is my daughter's championship soccer game. We won't be back until 10:00 or so. Why?"*

Frank has told me he is busy that evening but is indeed interested in why I am asking. In this case, because I told him I only had a few seconds; I can end the call quickly, letting him know we will talk again soon:

Ron: *"No biggie. I'll catch you another time - I've got to run - let's touch base next week."*

Acquaintances:

It is likely that your calls to acquaintances will come as a surprise, for they do not hear from you as often as a good friend would, if at all. So the reaction and/or comfort level will be different. With an acquaintance, you should make it clear right away that this is not a social call but rather a call with a specific purpose.

When calling an acquaintance, ask the prospect up front if your call has come at a bad time. This will indicate whether you should continue with the call. If the answer indicates you have called at a good time, your prospect has given you control and shown openness to your message.

If you called at a bad time, you can end the call quickly, leaving the door open to call back.

Ron: *"Hi Don, this is Ron Baker. We met at Sally and Rick's wedding last week."*

Don: *"Hello, how are you?"*

Ron: *"I'm great. Did I catch you at a bad time?"*

Here are a couple of subtle points. First, after the greeting, Don asked a common question, *"How are you?"*, almost as a natural reaction. He may not actually be interested as most likely he is just asking out of habit. Do not take this as an invitation to reminisce about the wedding you both attended, talk about children's soccer or otherwise go down the road of non-business chit-chat. As when speaking to a good friend, once your conversation turns social it will be difficult to bring it back to business. In this example, by answering Don's question quickly with, *"I'm great"* and then immediately saying, *"Did I catch you at a bad time?"*, I established control.

Asking the question *"Did I catch you at a bad time?"* forces Don to respond and in turn maintains both the direction and control of the conversation. If Don is free to talk, you move on to the next step. If it is not a good time to talk, he will most likely look forward with interest to the next call.

Referral:

Similar to calling an acquaintance, do not ask or respond to the phrase, *"How are you?"* In this case, your prospects do not know you and can consider your question about their well being as insincere.

If they happen to ask how you are, remember that this is a statement made out of habit. Resist the temptation to enter into idle chit-chat.

Demonstrate respect for the prospects' time by asking if they are able to speak. Take the time to offer a compliment that edifies your prospect. It is a good idea to say things relevant to prospects' strengths and factual about their personal lives, professional achievements or positive attributes.

You should have confirmed this information from the person who referred you to them before noting it on your prospect form found in the Forms Section in the back of the book.

Example:

Ron: *"Don, we have not been introduced but we have a common friend in Bob Hall. My name is Ron Baker."*

Don: *"Hello, Ron Baker. How is our good friend Robert?"*

Ron: *"Bob is great. He tells me you own the best printing plant in Fairbanks. Is that so?"*

Don: *"Oh, that's nice of him to say."*

Ron: *"Listen, I am glad I caught you. Did I reach you at a bad time?"*

The compliment is followed immediately by a question that requires Don to answer, thereby continuing the conversation. I obviously know a bit about Don and have taken a keen interest in him. Remember, the initial credibility established by your common association can be short-lived if you appear to have taken improper advantage of the association by sounding too casual.

You are better off staying a bit more formal until you develop a rapport with your referral. These subtle changes to a script can make the difference between moving to the next step with a prospect who is open and at ease, versus a prospect who is less open and a bit on edge.

"Effort only fully releases its reward after the person refuses to quit."

— NAPOLEON HILL

Chapter Six

STEER™ Element No. 3:
Enthusiastically Assume
the Appointment

Now you are ready to ask for the appointment. Remember you are competing with other activities for time and mind share. You have to demonstrate quickly to your prospects that their investment of time to meet with you will benefit them.

The overriding principle here is to decrease the emphasis of the perceived time investment while increasing interest in what will be gained from the meeting. The prospects must begin to feel they have something to gain from the meeting and something to lose by not taking the time to see you.

Let's return to our Good Friend example from the previous chapter, and presume the knowledge that Frank is open next Tuesday at 7:00:

Ron: *"Great, I have a business idea to run by you and I'd like to get your opinion on it. Put a pot of coffee on and I'll see you at 7:00."*

In this example, I am promoting a business venture. It could be a sub/pizza shop or a home-based business. It really doesn't matter; the dialogue works well in any case.

What makes this work is that Frank knows I want to discuss business, his opinion is of value to me, and he should have a pot of coffee ready by 7:00. Frank does not feel threatened because I only want to run these ideas by him to gain his opinion.

Because I <u>Cleared His Availability</u> up front, Frank will most likely not make the familiar *"I'm tied up"* excuse.

Now let's return to the Acquaintance example, continuing the dialogue with the assumption that we do not know Don's availability:

Ron: *"We were talking at the wedding about our old football injuries coming back to haunt us, and you mentioned how your joints really bother you at the end of the day. This may be a shot in the dark, but I'd like to show you something I've found that works great for me! What days next week are you tied up for lunch? It would be great to see you again."*

Here are a few subtle points that make this dialogue effective. In addition to stating the benefit of less pain from his football injuries, I helped Don <u>Clear His Availability</u> by asking what days next week he would <u>not</u> be available for lunch. Notice I did not ask what days he <u>was</u> available, instead asking what days he already had something scheduled. People are more aware of when they are busy than when they have free time. For example, think for a moment about when *you* are tied up next week. Most likely your mind will immediately scan your weekly calendar and create a picture of the times you are booked, leaving any free time obvious. This occurs because people tend to be more mentally busy than calendar busy.

Special Note: It is important that your words paint a mental picture so that your prospect sees the need for a face-to-face meeting. Saying *"I'd like to tell you about the details"* does not paint the picture of a meeting. Saying *"I'd like to show you the numbers"* paints the picture that your prospect must see your presentation

When I state my purpose to share a product with Don, I do not pause but rather continue on, assuming the appointment. A pause at this point would open the door for Don to suggest something other than a meeting. He may ask to be referred to a Web site or perhaps to be mailed information. Continuing the dialogue without pausing, and assuming the appointment, greatly increases the chance that he will agree to meet. Ending the dialogue by saying it would be great to see him again can add to his comfort level, supposing that he enjoyed my company at the wedding.

Now we return to the Referral example:

Ron: *"Don, my company specializes in saving mid to large printing plants up to 35 percent on their industrial cleaning supplies. Don, I'd like to sit down and see if we can do the same for you – are there any days next week where you would <u>not</u> be available for 20 minutes or so?"*

Notice how I make a point to repeat my prospect's name a couple of times during the call. The sweetest sound to someone's ears is his or her own name. This is amplified when someone unknown to us takes the time to speak our name during a brief call. This goes a long way toward keeping the prospect focused on the conversation.

I told Don that my company saves companies like his serious money on their industrial cleaning supplies and that I would like to *see* if I can do the same for him. I helped Don <u>Clear His Availability</u> by asking if there were any days he would not be available to meet for 20 minutes to find out.

"Try, try, try
and keep trying
is the rule that
must be followed
to become an expert
at anything"

— W. CLEMET STONE

Chapter Seven

STEER™ Element No. 4: Expect Then Manage Appointment Pushback

Notice that Element No. 4 is titled <u>Expect Then Manage Appointment Pushback</u>. You can almost always <u>expect</u> initial resistance to your request for an appointment from both qualified and unqualified prospects. The key is to properly <u>manage</u> this initial pushback to determine if your prospect's resistance indicates they are really not qualified or if it is just an <u>automatic response</u> from an otherwise qualified prospect. This initial resistance to an appointment is normal, welcomed and easily managed.

Why Is Appointment Pushback Normal?

Our lives are busy. Most of us instinctively avoid additional time commitments. As consumers, many of us react with simple knee jerk responses like, *"No thanks; I'm not interested right now,"* or *"I'm just looking"* when we think someone may want to sell us something or ask us to commit to a meeting. Similarly, prospects' initial resistance to an appointment is often nothing more than an <u>automatic response</u> to keep a safe distance. Knee-jerk reactions are common for both qualified and unqualified prospects.

You should look forward to Appointment Pushback. It offers valuable clues, and here is why. If every phone call you make results in an unchallenged appointment, the chances of meeting with <u>only</u>

qualified prospects is about zero. Without this pushback, you would find yourself quite busy and your calendar would be full — and your wallet would be empty. Wasting time meeting with unqualified prospects is just that: a waste of time. Think about it: Which would you prefer - mere activity, or activity with results?

What Are Common Appointment Pushback Types?

Appointment Pushback will fall into one of the following five categories:

- Status Quo Response: *"I am happy the way things are. No need to change or even to think about changing."*

- No Time Response: *"I don't have time for this right now. Maybe when my schedule settles down."*

- Brush-Off Response: *"Send me some information, and I'll get back to you if I am interested."*

- Rude Response: *"Are you kidding? I wouldn't be interested in anything like that!"*

- Tell Me More Response: *"Sure, sounds good, but can you give me some details now?"*

Let's look at each category in more detail.

Status Quo Response:

This response is frequently used by prospects who believe they already have what you offer, or feel they are happy with the way things are. You will know that you are dealing with the Status Quo Response when you hear things like *"I'm covered,"* or *"Our equipment works just fine,"* or *"I'm happy using XYZ brand."*

No Time Response:

This usually comes from someone who *feels* too busy to add anything significant to the schedule. It will sound like *"I'm booked for the next few weeks,"* or *"This week is bad for me,"* or *"This is a busy time of year for us."*

Brush-Off Response:

This response is most often used when your prospect does not take you or your offering seriously. The Brush-Off Response goes something like this: *"Can you send me some information?"*, or *"Do you have a Web site I can look at?"*, or *"Send me some literature, and if I am interested, I'll get back to you."* Typically, when a prospect says *"can you send me some information"*, they are thinking, *"I want to get off the phone now"*. When they say *"I'll look it over and get back to you"*, they are really saying *"I'll ignore it and never get back to you"*.

Rude Response:

This kind of response should never be taken personally. Often times a Rude Response comes from someone who simply lacks basic social skills or has been caught at a really bad time.

Tell Me More Response:

The Tell Me More Response is when your prospect asks for more details about your offering before agreeing to a meeting. This response is motivated by one of two reasons: either your prospect wishes to continue the conversation out of sincere interest, or wants more information to assess if what you want to talk about is worth the time. In either case, you are being asked to provide an abbreviated presentation on the spot. You know you are dealing with a Tell Me More Response when you hear something like, *"What can you tell about it now?"*, or *"Let's hear the details,"* or *"How does this compare to ABC?"*.

Appointment Pushback Management

Over the years, I have found that all <u>qualified</u> prospects share at least one of the following three traits. In general (and for the moment I must speak in general terms), a qualified prospect wants to be perceived as being:

1. Well-informed, knowledgeable and/or business savvy.
2. Courteous and likeable.
3. Fair to others.

Think of it this way: people who don't meet any of the above criteria disqualify themselves. You can then move on, knowing you have saved yourself time, money and aggravation.

Appointment Pushback is easily managed by following a few simple steps. This section illustrates these simple yet powerful principles through a fictional example of an individual commenting negatively on one of my favorite ties. Unbeknownst to him, this tie was a gift from my 9-year-old daughter. We are going to tackle the Rude Response to illustrate Appointment Pushback principles. This individual posing as the fashion police delivers a Rude Response to my invitation to attend a father/child home wardrobe party.

Acknowledge and Absorb the Pushback

When met with a prospect's resistance, the last thing you want to do is to dismiss the fact that your prospect has raised an issue or in any way respond to your prospect's initial pushback in a defensive manner. Acknowledging the concern tells the prospect that you recognize that the concern is valid from the prospect's point of view. This does not mean you agree with the prospect, as agreeing gives unnecessary power to the objection. Absorbing the objection tells your prospect that you are not rattled by their comment and do not take offense to it.

Ron: *"Fred, It's Ron Baker calling, we met at our daughters' soccer game last week."*

Fred: *"Oh, yes, how are you doing?"*

Ron: *"I'm great; listen, I only have a couple of seconds, did I get you at a bad time?"*

Fred: *"No, what can I do for you?"*

Ron: *"Fred, may I ask you what your plans are for Tuesday evening"?*

Fred: *"I have nothing scheduled. Why?"*

Ron: *"Fred, I am having a father/child get-together next Tuesday evening at 7:00. It's a men's wardrobe party where children get to pick out a special tie as a Father's Day gift - we would love to have you and Sarah join us."*

Fred: *"That sounds interesting, but Ron, I've got to tell you, I have seen you wear some of the ugliest ties I have ever seen. Is your daughter color blind?"*

Need I mention that this is a rude response?

Answering this pushback by saying something like, *"No they aren't, and she isn't!"* or *"I don't agree with you!"*, neither absorbs nor acknowledges Fred's rude response. At this point, it's one person's opinion against another.

However, I can choose to take a different approach by saying something like, *"I know what you mean"* (Acknowledge). *I get that a lot when I wear that yellow goose tie"* (Absorb). This approach tells prospects that they are not the only ones who think this way and that you understand their point of view.

Illuminate the Positive Traits Shared by Qualified Prospects

While restating the benefits of your offering, illuminate the positive traits shared by most qualified prospects. A prospect may not fully understand what good will comes from agreeing to a meeting with you. In addition to listing these benefits, it is a good idea to remind your prospects that they are likeable, business-savvy and fair individuals, and therefore should be open to looking at the benefits your offering can bring.

Continuing with our ugly-tie example, I can respond with:

Ron: *"Fred, an involved parent like you knows that it's the little things that mean so much to children* (Knowledgeable), *and I know how going the extra mile for a smile comes naturally to you* (Likeable). *Imagine the look in your little girl's eyes when she sees you go out the door wearing a tie she picked out just for you* (Benefit). *You may get some comments from time to time, but her memories* (Benefit) *seem worthwhile, don't you think?"* (Fair)

After that, do you think Fred really sees an ugly tie, or perhaps now wants one of his own?

Re-invite

Re-invite the prospect by expressing with limited risk the need for a face-to-face appointment. At this point, your prospects believe that you understand their objection, have been reminded of their positive traits, and more clearly understand what benefits they may enjoy if they take the time to see you. Now, your prospect may be more open to your request for a meeting. Re-state the need for a face-to-face appointment, illustrating how a small time investment may yield significant benefits.

Ron: *"We are getting together at my house Tuesday evening from 7:00 to 7:30.* (Small Time Investment) *I'd really enjoy seeing you and Sara there. Can I count on you?*

Evaluate

Listen to the prospect's response. If your prospect agrees to your second invitation, you should immediately move on to secure the appointment. If your prospect does not respond positively, respectfully end the call. You can then move on to your next prospect, glad that you saved yourself both time and money.

"I wouldn't wear a tie that looks like that no matter who gave it to me," would be a reply that clearly plants this prospect in the <u>unqualified</u> category. Next!

Those who manage pushback well and secure appointment after appointment with qualified prospects have mastered the ability to remind prospects just how well informed, likeable and fair they really are,(after first acknowledging and then absorbing their initial resistance). It does not matter if you want to meet with a prospect about a million-dollar computer system, discuss life-insurance needs, or explain the benefits of a home-based business. These principles will work no matter what your appointment is about.

Prospects who ultimately sit down with you will thank you for managing their initial pushback and helping them see the value of your offering. Remember, you have something of value to share, and have the best interests of your prospects in mind. Managing their initial resistance to an appointment helps them see the value of your offering. If done properly, they will indeed thank you.

Now let's look at how these Pushback Management principles can be used more practically. We will continue on with the Good Friend, Acquaintance and Referral examples dialogue begun earlier.

No Time Example (Good Friend):

Frank: *"Hey, listen, this is a busy time for me. My plate is full right now."*

Ron: *"I know what you mean.* (Acknowledge) *Between work and the kids, I have never been busier myself.* (Absorb) *Listen, this project is important and I really value your point of view.* (Business Savvy) *There may be something in it for you as well.* (Benefit) *How about we grab a 20-minute cup of coffee.* (Re-invite; Small Time Investment) *I'll show you some of the highlights and you tell me what you think.* (Business Savvy) *If it looks good, we can get together again. Worst case, Frank, we spend 20 minutes over coffee - does that sound fair?"* (Fair)

In this example, my good friend Frank hit me with a No Time Response. Notice that my reply points out that I regard Frank as a business-savvy individual who may benefit from a small time investment. At worst case, two good friends get together over coffee. The dialogue is conversational and is in no way pushy. It would ot put my good friend on the defensive. Doesn't that sound fair to you?

Brush-Off Example (Acquaintance):

Don: *"I have tried all kinds of supplements and find they really don't seem to work well. Besides, the prices are through the roof — but thanks anyway."*

Ron: *"I know exactly what you mean.* (Acknowledge) *I have looked and looked myself.* (Absorb) *You can imagine how thrilled I was to finally find something that gives me some relief!* (Benefit) *You have really got to see what XYZ has done to make their products effective - they really are different.* (Be Informed) *Let's grab a quick lunch next week* (Re-invite; Small Time Investment) *and I'll bring the information for you to look at, and you be the judge.* (Knowledgeable) *If you think it's worth a try, great. If not, no biggie - besides, it would be great to see you again.* (Likeable) *Does that sound fair?"* (Fair)

Status Quo Example (Referral):

Don: *"I think we are all set for now. We get our supplies from Universal Supply Co. We've been with them for years, but thank you for calling."*

Ron: *"Universal does a great job.* (Acknowledge) *I actually compete with them often.* (Absorb) *My customers find our prices and online order tracking to be a real business advantage.* (Benefit) *I'm not sure how much money we may be able to save you,* (Be Informed) *but it would take only a few moments to find out.* (Small Time Investment) *When we sit down,* (Re-invite) *I can put together a few numbers and show you how we will compete for your business.* (Business Savvy) *If we don't measure up, we are only out a few minutes.* (Small Time Investment) *Does that sound fair?"* (Fair)

Tell Me More Example (Good Friend):

Frank: *"Sure, but can you tell me what this is all about?"*

Ron: *"Absolutely.* (Acknowledge) *Remember last month when we were tossing around our concerns about coming up with enough money to pay for the kids' college?"*

Frank: *"Yes, I remember."*

Ron: *"Well, I came across an idea that I believe can help both of us with the kids' college funds,* (Benefit) *and I need to run the numbers by you."* (Business Savvy) *Frank, worst-case scenario we'll have some coffee together - fair enough?"* (Fair)

Notice that you can apply these objection management techniques to virtually any appointment setting situation. It is important that you understand, prepare and rehearse these techniques with dialogue specific to your particular offering.

"But what do I do if the prospect asks a question I haven't thought of or am not prepared for?"

It is possible that you may get a question you feel does not fall into one of these pushback categories. When this occurs, your response should be to:

1. Acknowledge your prospect's question.
2. Maintain control of the call.

I have found this response very effective when confronted with an objection I have not heard before:

"Good question. This is the first time I've been asked that. Let me do some research and I'll have an answer for you when we get together."

In this example, I don't shy away from the question or let the prospect think I do not want to answer the concern. I acknowledge that the question is a good one-I simply don't have an answer at the moment.

"Every strike brings me closer to my next home run"

— Babe Ruth

Chapter Eight

STEER™ Element No. 5: Reaffirm After Confirming Date, Time and Location

It would be a tragedy if either you or your prospect makes a mistake about the time or place of your meeting. Confirming, and reaffirming your appointment is well worth the effort and will save you a lot of time. The appointment date, time and location are key. The following dialogue works well for any prospect type:

Ron: *"OK, that's 10:00 Tuesday the 5th in your office at 34 South University Avenue."* (Confirm)

Prospect: *"Yes, that's right."*

Ron: *"Great, I am writing in my calendar 10:00 next Tuesday at your office on South University."* (Reaffirm)

In this example, the prospect has heard the day and date (Tuesday the 5th) twice; the time (10 a.m.) twice; and the location (his office on South University) twice as well. Each critical schedule component has been reaffirmed, leaving no room for error. Saying that you are writing this information into your calendar as you speak helps the prospect realize that the appointment is now written in stone.

Customizing scripts using STEER™ gives you

Five Power Advantages:

- **Power Advantage One:** You will sound comfortable and confident in what you are saying because the words are yours. Your prospect will be at ease because you are.

- **Power Advantage Two:** You will be in the driver's seat, steering your prospect to the appointment.

- **Power Advantage Three:** You will be able to communicate several compelling reasons why your prospect should meet with you.

- **Power Advantage Four:** You will have prepared for common Appointment Pushback. Resistance to an appointment can be managed comfortably and confidently.

- **Power Advantage Five:** You will never have misunderstandings concerning the date, place and time of your meetings

In the Forms section in the back of the book, you will find several blank Custom Script Builder forms. This is the tool for you to use in customizing specific dialogue for the purpose of making contact with and inviting current and potential clients to explore doing business with you. As you know by now, for success to occur, you must routinely call on prospects to set face-to-face appointments, invite them to attend workshops, open houses and/or webcasts. Use these forms as a template to insure that you don't leave out any steps along the way. Remember, each person that agrees to meet with you, brings you closer to your goal. Each successful appointment begins the process that results in more business. Taking shortcuts or *winging it* will cost money. Take this process seriously.

Following STEER™ to the letter will give you the best chance that your calls with be easy for you to make and easy for those you call to stay open to hearing what you have to say.

Tips for Scripts

Simply write down in your own words what you will say for each prospect and meeting type. Follow the Form, making sure you include each element in your approach.

Notice that the space provided to develop dialogue for managing Appointment Pushback is located on a separate Form. Simply lay both sheets of paper side by side so that all the information required for these calls is right in front of you. Having a written custom script along with a response for each pushback type right at your fingertips will add to your confidence and effectiveness. You will reap the dividends for years to come.

On pages 68-73 are six completed sample forms for your review. Notice that the scripts are not written word for word; nor should you read your scripts word for word when making calls. Use <u>Word Cues</u> instead. Here's why.

It is very hard for someone to read verbatim any script over the phone and not sound as if they are reading something already prepared. You may have received calls from time to time where you felt that the person was not actually speaking to <u>you,</u> but rather reciting a pre-staged sales approach. Most likely you became uncomfortable, and your attention was diverted away from what the caller was saying and instead you became focused on how to most quickly end the call.

Avoid this by using key words and phrases to trigger what you are going to say. For example if you see the word <u>Time</u> written in the Take Control section of the Script Builder Form, your mind should immediately go to the phrase *"I hope I haven't caught you at a bad time."* The words should roll off your tongue as they would during normal conversation rather than sounding like a prepared sales pitch.

Take a moment and complete the following Exercise. Below you will find the beginning of several popular phrases. Write down at the end of each line the first words that come to mind.

Take me out to the _____ _____

Little Miss Muffet _____ _____ _____ _____

What goes up _____ _____ _____

E= _____

How to Win Friends _____ _____ _____

Rich Dad _____ _____

The Hatfields and _____

Fred Astaire and _____ _____

It's only _____ _____
(Hint: this may be new, but just as important!)

Did you say *Take me out to the* **(Ball Game)**;
Little Miss Muffet **(sat on her tuffet)**;
What goes up **(must come down)**;
E= **(MC2)**;
How to Win Friends **(and Influence People)**;
Rich Dad **(Poor Dad)**;
The Hatfields **(and McCoys)**;
Fred Astaire **(and Ginger Rodgers)**;
and of course, last but not least, you should know by now,
It's only **(Cheese Cloth!)**

Word Cues work well to trigger your normal tone and conversational voice. You will sound confident, certain and as if you have been contacting and inviting for years.

Custom Script Builder
Good Friend

Set at Ease

> Statement of Familiarity

Hey Joe

It's Ron

Take Control

> Confirm Prospect is open to talk

Got a second?

Clear Tuesday or Thursday @ 7:00 PM

Ethusiastically Assume Appointment

Found a Way

Kids college fund

Web Cast @ 7:00

> Increase Interest – decrease time commitment

Put $ away without going Broke

You must See it

1 hour + Questions

Expect then Manage Pushback ⟹

Reaffirm after Confirming

> Write it in Stone

Great! Tuesday @ 7:00

My Place

Writing it down for Tuesday @ 7:00

See you then

Expect then Manage Pushback

Good Friend

Status Quo

Good for you.

> No Need!
> I am already happy!

That's Great

Your opinion is important

See what I got

Less than an hour – sound fair?

No Time

Understand

> I don't have time
> to look!

Never busier myself

Your opinion is important

Little time to find out

Help me – sound fair?

Brush Off

Sure!

> Send me some info.
> I'll get back to you.

Have researched myself

Need to see my analysis

Will show you over coffee

Your opinion is important

Less than an hour – sound fair?

Tell Me More

Love to

> Tell me all the
> details Now!

I've crunched numbers

See my analysis / explain my numbers

Your opinion is important

Less than an hour – sound fair?

Custom Script Builder
Acquaintance

Set at Ease

Don Parker?

Statement of Familiarity

Ron Baker Calling

Sally and Rick's wedding last Saturday

Take Control

Bad Time?

Confirm Prospect is open to talk

Ethusiastically Assume Appointment

Old football injuries

finally some relief

Increase Interest – decrease time commitment

days lunch booked next week?

great to see you

Expect then Manage Pushback

Reaffirm after Confirming

Great! Day, Date, Location, Time

Write it in Stone

Writing in my calender

Day, Date, Location, Time

See you then

Expect then Manage Pushback

Acquaintance

Status Quo

Good for you.

That's Great

Your opinion is important

See what I got

Good to have lunch – sound fair?

> No Need!
> I am already happy!

No Time

Understand

Never busier myself

Your opinion is important

Little time to find out

Good to have lunch – sound fair?

> I don't have time
> to look!

Brush Off

Sure!

Have researched myself

Works well for me

Will show you over coffee

Your opinion is important

Sound fair?

> Send me some info.
> I'll get back to you.

Tell Me More

Love to

I feel great

Finally results

Show you what I have

Good to have lunch– sound fair?

> Tell me all the
> details Now!

Custom Script Builder
Referral

Set at Ease

Statement of Familiarity

Don Spenser

Rob Hall reffered

Coach Soccer

Take Control

Confirm Prospect is open to talk

Glad to speak to you

Reach @ bad time?

Ethusiastically Assume Appointment

Save money

Industrial Supplies

Increase Interest – decrease time commitment

35%

Do same for you

Not available next week?

Expect then Manage Pushback
Reaffirm after Confirming

Great! Date, Time

Write it in Stone

Location

Writing in my calender

Day, Location, Time

See you then

Expect then Manage Pushback
Referral

Status Quo

> No Need!
> I do business with
> someone else

XYZ is a fine company

Compete often

Current customer advantage

Show you numbers

You be the judge – sound fair?

No Time

> I don't have time
> to look!

Understand

Never busier myself

Little time to exchange business cards

Know who to call when need arises

Great to meet you – sound fair?

Brush Off

> Send me some info.
> I'll get back to you.

Sure!

Customer testamonials

Show you our advantage

Know who to call when need arises

Great to meet you – sound fair?

Tell Me More

> Tell me all the
> details Now!

Love to

Customer testamonials

Show you our advantage

Exchange business cards

Great to meet you

Exchange business cards – sound fair?

"Most of our
obstacles would
melt away if,
instead of cowering
before them, we
should make up our
minds to walk
boldly through
them."

— Orison Swett Marden

Chapter Nine

Handling Gatekeepers and Voicemail

But What About Gatekeepers?

Gatekeepers are those people who stand between you and your prospect. They frequently screen incoming calls to protect the prospect's time, either at home or at work. Gatekeepers fall into two main categories: Corporate or Company Gatekeepers (administrative assistant, receptionist or subordinate); or what I call a Domestic Gatekeeper (spouse, child or baby sitter). The likelihood that a gatekeeper will be the person answering the phone is quite high. Gatekeepers, particularly those in an office environment, take their screening responsibilities quite seriously. Have you ever called a prospect and had your call answered by a Gatekeeper? If so, perhaps the conversation went something like this?

Sam: *"Hello, Is Mrs. Smith available?"*
Gatekeeper: *"Who is calling?"*
Sam: *"My name is Sam Francisco, I just need to speak with her for a moment."*
Gatekeeper: *"And, what is this in reference to?"*
Sam: *"Well, I was talking to Susan Jackson the other day, and she mentioned that Mrs. Smith might be open to looking at ...."*
(interrupted)
Gatekeeper: *"Susan Jackson, I'm not sure I know a Susan Jackson. What did you say your name was?"*

Sam: *"Sam Francisco. May I speak with Mrs. Smith please?"*
Gatekeeper: *"I don't think she will be interested, besides she is busy right now. I'll tell her you called."*
Sam: *"Great, my number is 518-981 541...."* (interrupted)
Gatekeeper: *"I've got your number on our caller ID. We'll know when you are calling back. Good Bye."*

Ouch!

In this case, the Gatekeeper was in control of the call from the start. Sam might just as well have said, *"I may not know Mrs. Smith, she may not know me, and she most likely will find my call a complete waste of time".* None of which are true. In fact, Carol Smith is on Sam's **"Acquaintance"** prospect list. Both she and Sam have played summer softball on the same local league for the past 10 years. The above dialogue leverages none of these facts and may have ruined a perfectly good prospect. In general, a Gatekeeper is primarily concerned with three things about your call. They are:

1. Who is calling?
2. Does the prospect know you?
3. Might your call be welcomed by and of value to your prospect?

A common myth about Gatekeepers is that they're primarily interested in _why_ you are calling. Frankly, more times than not, they are less concerned about the topic of your call, than they are concerned about protecting your prospect's time. They protect the prospect by screening unwelcome callers.

Your goal is to gain their approval so that they quickly pass your call on to your prospect. It is safe to say that the longer the gatekeeper interrogates you, the less the chance that you will reach your prospect.

Make it <u>easy</u> for them to pass your call on to the prospect. How? Answer their concerns upfront. Let them know who you are and how the prospect will know you. Speak with poise, posture and confidence, giving little doubt that your call will be of value. This will go along way towards putting them at ease, and in turn increase the probability that your call will passed on to your prospect unchallenged.

For example:
Sam: *"Hi, this is Sam Francisco, I play softball with Carol. Could you please get her for me? Thanks!"*

In this example, three distinct components <u>make it easy</u> for the Gatekeeper to pass on Sam's call. First he stated his name up front answering the question: *"Who is calling?"*; followed immediately by how the prospect may know him (Carol and Sam play in the same softball league, therefore she would welcome the call). Sam ended the dialogue with a call to action, specifically instructing the Gatekeeper what to do next. By ending the request by saying *"thanks"*,

Sam assumes his request will be honored without further discussion or questioning by the gatekeeper. He is in control from *"Hello!"* (This is Posture)

<u>Gatekeeper Guidelines</u>:

Prefixes:
It's important that the Gatekeeper is set at ease. Therefore, whenever possible, refer to your intended prospect <u>without</u> the use of formal greetings such as Mr., Mrs., Ms or Dr. The use of such prefixes screams *"stranger calling"* to the Gatekeeper, and communicates that you <u>do not</u> have a comfortable or familiar relationship with the prospect. This will propel even the most mild mannered

person into *super gatekeeper mode!* Whenever possible, I recommend using your prospect's first name only.

Call to Action:

In a relaxed and confident tone, request that the Gatekeeper call your prospect to the phone. End your request by saying *"thank you"*. This will indicate the expectation that they will honor your request without any further resistance and/or any additional small talk.

Conversational Dialogue:

Note that my dialogue in the previous example makes use of everyday, conversational language; i.e. could you *"get"* her for me? If I were to use formal words, for example: *"could you summon her to the phone?"*, chances are it would raise a red flag of suspicion and put the Gatekeeper on high alert. Your goal is to communicate in a style that reflects a caller who would be not only welcomed but expected. Note that I use the least amount of words possible to make the request. The aim is to speak with a tone and pace that sounds conversational and personable, as if you have made a social call to this individual one hundred times before. This will go a long way in increasing the probability that your request will be passed along with minimum resistance. This will take practice; but the results will be empowering and extremely rewarding. Chapter Eleven will introduce powerful strategies to enhance the preparation of all your prospecting efforts.

Maximizing Your Effectiveness with a Referral

If a referral name can be referenced during your call, you will find that this serves well to set the Gatekeeper at ease, assuming the gatekeeper is familiar with the referring party. The more recognizable the referral's name is to the Gatekeeper, the better. Always speak in a comfortable and confident manner with the assumption that the Gatekeeper will recognize the referral's name or a common association. By doing so you will quickly establish in the

Gatekeeper's mind that you are familiar with the prospect and that they (the prospect) would be delighted to take your call.

For example:
Ron: *"Hello, Ron Baker calling. Paul Young from Carol's softball team suggested that I give a Carol a call. Please tell Carol I'm calling. Thank you!"*

The above technique will be effective if you are confident that the Gatekeeper will recognize the party who referred the prospect. However, if the gatekeeper is not familiar with the name of the person who referred you to the prospect, you may receive pushback.

For example:
Gatekeeper: *"I'm sorry. I don't think I know Paul Young."* (Gatekeeper Pushback)

In this case, it is critical that you are armed with accurate information that will illuminate the association between the referring party and the prospect. This is covered in detail later in the chapter titled *Supercharge Your Prospect List.*

Ron: *"Oh, Carol and Paul play softball together."*

On occasion, a Gatekeeper will request further information.

Perhaps out of habit alone they may say something like:*"May I ask what this is about?"*, thus giving additional pushback. At this point, you may want to make clear that your call is important and would be sadly missed if the prospect was not called to the phone.

For Example:
Ron: *"Paul and I are working on a project and want to make sure Carol is not left out. We want to keep her in the loop. Is she there?"*

The principle is to communicate to the Gatekeeper that by not passing the phone to Carol, she will be excluded from an important conversation or event. The risk of disappointing Carol is high.

An invaluable technique as a tool of preparation for pushback of all kinds, including that of a Gatekeeper, is to journal the specific pushback received when making calls. Using the principles you have learned in this and the previous chapters, you will be able to properly prepare for, and handle effectively, the pushback that you receive. Preparation and practice are vital. I cannot overstate the importance of being prepared for a Gatekeeper's pushback as you would if you had reached to prospect directly. As with all pushback, it should be anticipated, and therefore can be prepared for and managed effectively.

A Special Note on Corporate Gatekeepers

It is not uncommon to find many professionals at work early, eating lunch at their desks, working after hours and occasionally coming into the office on a Saturday. Most Corporate or Company Gatekeepers work normal business hours from 8 a.m. to 5 p.m. taking either an hour or half-hour for lunch. These are prime times to call, as your prospect is now unguarded. A time-tested technique successfully used to bypass corporate or company gatekeepers is to call during off-hours to catch prospects unguarded. Before 7:30 a.m., at exactly 12:15 p.m., after 5:30 p.m. or on Saturdays at 11:00 a.m. are prime times to catch prospect at their desk.

Placing a call directly to your prospect during unguarded times greatly increase your chances that the prospect will actually pick up the phone. For this technique to work, you will need to obtain your prospect's direct-dial number. You can usually get a person's work direct-dial number simply by calling the main company switchboard and asking the receptionist; or when calling on a larger firm, this information is often given freely by the company's accounts receivable department. They actually welcome incoming calls and are not trained to screen requests for directory information.

In some cases, you won't be able to avoid speaking with the Corporate Gatekeeper. Corporate Gatekeepers are like any other human being in that they love to hear the sound of their own name and they rarely hear the words *"thank you"*. Whenever possible, learn the correct pronunciation of the Corporate Gatekeeper's name. The correct pronunciation of the Corporate Gatekeeper's name can be obtained by calling the company switchboard as well.

Like Domestic Gatekeepers, it is important that the Corporate Gatekeeper knows who you are and that your call would be welcomed by your prospect.

Here's an example:
Ron: *"Hello, Sue Smith. Ron Baker calling for Jim. Our daughters play on the same soccer team, and I only need a moment, thank you."*

In this example, the Gatekeeper is greeted with both first and last name, and if possible, reference an association of familiarity. This will differentiate this call from the countless others the Gatekeeper receives on a daily basis.

What if I just can't get through?

The addition of cell phone technology has added a great advantage to our ability to contact and communicate with others at times when it was previously impossible. With a little knowledge and preparation, cell phones can offer this same advantage when it comes to aiding our efforts to reach our prospects, and avoiding traditional barriers such as Gatekeepers.

The Gatekeeper may often tell you that your prospect is not available, is currently out, or has just left. If the Gatekeeper informs you that the prospect is currently not on the premises, confidently ask the Gatekeeper: *"Can I reach them on their cell phone?"* The Gatekeeper will often give you the prospect's cell phone number as they often do not have the technology to forward your call.

Whenever Possible, Be Proactive:

The more phone numbers that you have to reach your prospect, the better the chances are that you will be able to reach them without the intervention of a Gatekeeper. A technique that I have used with great success since the introduction of the cell phone, is that when making my initial introduction to a prospect or during the development of my prospect list, I make it a point to gather every bit of information that I can about them – including every possible phone number where they could be reached. I ask every new contact that I consider a possible prospect for their business card, which often lists many numbers including that of a cell phone. Always take a glance at a business card when you receive it and if it does not have a cell phone number on it, casually hand the card back to the prospect and say, *"can you put your cell number on the back for me?"* I have found that most agree to my request without objection.

In addition, always carry business cards of your own as well as a pen. You will often meet people who may have the potential to be a great prospect, yet are without a business card at the time. The solution is to hand them one of your cards with a pen, and request that they provide their contact information on the back of it. Without this simple yet important habit, there is the risk that you may lose the advantage of these potentially valuable introductions.

A Few Words on Voicemail:

I remember back in the early '80s when my company installed

voicemail into our office phone system. At first, I thought, *"this is great. I'll never miss another call. My customers and prospects can just leave a voice message that I can save, transfer to another colleague, or just delete. What a great idea!"* Then I realized that in addition to being a great message-taker for me, a voicemail system is also a great Gatekeeper for my customers and prospects and one that is tough to get around.

I quickly learned that to get past voicemail, I needed some new strategies. A typical voice mail system usually does allow us to leave a quick message. If the message is compelling, you will likely get a return call. If you never get a call back, don't worry; just move on down your list. Don't waste time leaving messages for someone who will not return your calls. A large prospect list makes makes moving on much easier. Please note that if some people are determined never to answer their phone personally or return a call, neither I nor anyone else can change that.

A few tips on leaving a voicemail message:

A prospect's voicemail system can sometimes work to your advantage. A well-constructed message left on your prospect's voice mail enables you to:

- Reach a prospect otherwise unreachable.
- Deliver your invitation for an appointment without objection or interruption.
- Make calls at off hours, enabling you to fill otherwise unproductive time.
- Receive a return call, which is an invitation for you to speak live with a prospect who has now expressed interest in speaking with you.

Components of an Effective Voicemail Message:

A voicemail script is similar to your previous scripts with a few subtle exceptions. Let's build a voicemail script for an acquaintance.

Set the Prospect at Ease:

Your voice may be unfamiliar to your prospects; therefore it is important that you take the time to set them at ease by stating right away how you received their name. With friends or acquaintances, don't waste time with idle chitchat. Start by stating up front your name and association:

"Hello Frank, Ron Baker calling. You may remember we met at Jack and Sally's wedding last Saturday."

Take Control:

When you speak into a recording device, you may think you are in control, but remember; your prospect can delete your message with a push of a single button. You need to establish control in such a way that compels the prospect to listen to your entire message. When leaving a message, don't be shy about saying you want to speak to your prospect <u>live</u>. It is important to make this known in your message. I like to give the prospect the opportunity to call me back:

"Frank, it's rather important we speak live. I'll try you back in about an hour, or feel free to call me at 555-555-1111. If my voice mail answers, leave a message with a best time and number to reach you directly."

In this example, I put some compelling information into just a few quick sentences. I told Frank that:

- We need to speak live. Merely leaving messages won't do.
- If he does not reach me when he calls back, he should leave a message with the best way for me to reach him directly.

If Frank uses Caller ID as a Gatekeeper, he may then see it is you calling and take the call. Maybe he will be compelled to give you his private cellphone number!

The following is an example of a voicemail message that works well if you're calling a referral. Note how this wording maximizes the principle of association. I have found this technique almost always prompts a return call:

"Frank, my name is Ron Baker and I am calling in regard to Paul Finnamore. I'll try you back in about an hour, or feel free to call me at 555-555-1111. If my voice mail answers, leave a message with a best time and number to reach you directly."

Reaffirm After Confirming.

Let your prospects know once again that you intend to call back at a specific time and that you look forward to speaking with them soon:

"Frank, I look forward to speaking with you soon. I'll try back in about an hour."

Your prospect now knows that you called about something important, you want to speak live and it is important that you do, and you intend to call back. The prospect can speed the process along by leaving a message with instructions on making direct contact.

In summary, effective voicemail messages have what I call The Three Cs: comfort, credibility and curiosity. I create comfort and credibility by using statements of familiarity (*"I am a friend of Paul Finnamore"*).

I create curiosity by keeping the message brief, omitting specific details of my offering or proposal. Leaving specific details concerning the purpose of your call, such as *"I'd like to speak with you regarding a business opportunity"*, gives your prospect just enough information to make an uninformed decision. A qualified prospect may end up taking steps to avoid your future calls.

Your goal is to communicate the purpose and value of your offering directly to the prospect. It is in your prospects' best interest to receive every chance to make informed decisions. To do that, they must speak with you live.

"You can't build a reputation on what you are *Going To Do!*"

— HENRY FORD

Chapter Ten

Supercharge
Your Prospect List

Like uncut diamonds buried deep beneath the earth, the potential jewels of your business lie in the natural resources of your prospect list. In this arena, the bigger the mine, the greater the potential for hitting the mother lode. In the following pages, you will quickly and easily learn how to develop, organize, and maintain an endless prospect list.

Big List Equals Big Potential

The number of names on your prospect list can directly affect your confidence level and attitude on the phone. For example, if you have 35 names on your list and you burn through 25 without much success (which won't happen if you properly use STEER™), you may get anxious and discouraged as your prospect reservoir disappears before your very eyes. However, if you have a solid list of 150 names and have the same results, you still have 125 names on your list. You can make the appropriate adjustments to your scripts and get back on the phone with plenty of prospects left.

During this initial phase of developing your list, <u>it's important that you do not leave off any names</u>. <u>Fight the urge to prejudge!</u> You may never contact some of the names on your list, but they can act as memory links or mental reference points to names of other viable prospects.

For example, let's say you think of your 85-year-old Uncle Joe, and your first thought is that Uncle Joe would not need or be interested in what you are offering. Do you still put him on your list? Yes! Because later, when you go over your initial list and see Uncle Joe's name, it might bring back the memory of a family event. Maybe you were playing cards with your Uncle Joe, and perhaps your cousin (who you had not thought of initially) was also playing. Now your cousin is added to your list. Thanks, Uncle Joe!

Organize for Results

The following exercises will effectively generate a large list of names that can be increased over time. Once your rough list has been made, you should then divide the names into specific categories. You'll find this helpful as you begin preparing for your calls.

These categories mirror the custom scripts you developed in Chapter Three:

A) Relatives and/or Good Friends:

These prospects are obviously the most familiar to you. Let's assume for now that your relationship with this population is warm, trusting and respectful.

B) Acquaintances:

These prospects will eventually make up a sizable portion of your working names list and will include people you interact with both professionally or casually during normal activities in any given month. This list would include your attorney, banker, accountant, doctor(s), dentist(s), chiropractor, kids' coaches, travel agent, hairdresser, dry cleaner, mail carrier, veterinarian, pharmacist, clergy, manicurist, teachers, delivery people, fellow churchgoers, fellow club members, former school chums, neighbors, etc., etc., etc.

C) Referrals:

These are good friends and acquaintances of your good friends and acquaintances — you have not met them yet. If you had met them, they would be on your Acquaintances list.

Go to the Prospect Forms in the back of the book. One is provided for each category – Good Friends, Acquaintances and Referrals. Notice the headings along the top of the forms. As you write down names, make sure you also write down all the information requested (name, phone number, referral source and association).

You can't count an entry as a prospect unless you have all the required information. In addition to the prospect's name and phone number, you will also need to write down your association or the person who referred you and their association with this prospect. This is important information to be used when developing your custom scripts.

You may think to yourself, *"But I don't know that many people".* By using the following formula, you need never speak those self-defeating words again! In a matter of 45 to 60 minutes, most anyone, usually to their amazement, can develop a list of 100, 200, even 300 names or more! You just need to know how.

Lists You Already Have

The quickest way to add names to your list is to simply go get the names. Yes, you read that right — simply go get the names! Chances are you already have more than one very detailed list of names complete with addresses and phone numbers. Do you have a personal address and phone book and/or Rolodex? Do you keep a birthday-card list, Christmas list, or Hanukkah list? If you are married, pull out your wedding list. Not the final wedding list, but the unabridged version, before you said, *"This many people would be nice but we don't have room for everyone."*

Alumni lists, church lists, association and club lists, fraternity/sorority lists, and military lists can all be worked with as is or with minimal updating. These suggestions will get you started.

Now continue building your list from less obvious, less prepared sources. If you're the type of individual who's not much on keeping the previously mentioned lists, you may think that building a list of over 100 names is impossible. It isn't-and here is how you do it.

Let Your Fingers Do The Walking

Sometimes the simplest tools can be the most effective. A common public phone book can be an incredibly powerful memory-jogging tool. It can be very useful in generating a list of prospects with whom you have had some affiliation. I am not recommending you open up the phone book and start making cold calls; this is simply a tool to jog your memory and help you create the initial list.

The following exercise, if done properly, will remind you of names of people from all areas of your past, as well as people of more recent association. Chances are that your pen or keyboard will have a difficult time keeping up. Here we go!

Go get your local Yellow Pages and turn to the A's for starters. Look at the first professional listing; let's say it's Abrasive Cutting Shops (a machine shop). You may know a few people who work in machine shops. One of them may actually own the business, which could be the largest in town. If your brain had not been triggered to think of Abrasive Cutting (machine shops), you most likely would not have thought of them. They would not have been added to your list. Continue through the listings — Accountants, Air Conditioning, Attorneys, etc. — until you get to that ever-popular listing: Zoologists.

Would you have thought of these names without the good old Yellow Pages? Go through each heading on every page and write down everyone who comes to mind.

Now, open your local White Pages. The quickest way to get the most complete, diversified list of *first* names is to turn to the most popular last name. For example, let's say that name is Smith. Begin with the first listing of Smith. Notice that each listing of Smith has a unique first name as well. The first listing may be Allen, followed by Arthur, Barbara and so on. As you read this list of first names you will be reminded of many people you've not seen or spoken to since high school. Remember, <u>do not prejudge.</u> Just write the names down as they come to you.

Note: Don't shortcut this process. By not taking the time to properly develop your initial list, you could potentially miss the opportunity to capitalize on a valuable business relationship that could improve both your and your prospect's life for years to come.

Oh, The Power of the Referral

One plus one equals five. New math? No, <u>referral math</u>. Every client is a referral source who can lead you to another client, who is a referral source who can lead to another client, who is a referral . . . well, you get the idea.

There are many good reasons to treat your clients with fairness, respect and with your best service. None of this manifests itself more in your wallet than the fact that every happy client is an opportunity for a valuable referral. It is imperative that you treat every prospect and existing client as if that person represents 100 referrals. They just may.

Work Hard to Be Referable

Always presenting yourself in a professional manner can pay

long-term dividends. When presenting your product, service and/or opportunity, treat people in a way that leaves them comfortable with you and your organization. If they are comfortable with you, then they will be more apt to feel that you will treat their friends or professional acquaintances with the same level of professionalism. Ideally, someone who gives the name of a referral should feel they have done a favor to the person they are referring to you.

Asking for the Referral

When you are with a prospect, don't miss the opportunity to build your prospect list. Ask and you shall receive is the elusive yet simple secret of gathering referrals. Rarely will an individual volunteer referral names. To get a referral, you must ask.

How you ask for a referral can also impact your success. Don't ask the person with whom you are speaking if they know anybody who would be in the market for any of your products, services or opportunity. Instead, start by asking for help.

"Joe, who do you know that might benefit from what we are talking about?"

Be sure to thank the referring person and let them know that you will keep them informed of the results. Be certain to follow up every time. It goes a long way toward strengthening your already good relationship and leaves the door open for future business and, of course, more referrals.

Effectively asking for referrals is a process for which you must be prepared and have practiced. When possible, you should test your method with an experienced coach, manager or colleague.

Keep the following points in mind:
1.   Prospect names are the natural resource of your business.

94

2. You may need to dig deep, sometimes really deep, to get to those diamonds beneath the surface.

3. Don't prejudge as you build your list; an unqualified prospect may very well lead you to your best prospect ever.

4. Treat every prospect with respect and professionalism. You never know whom they know and whom they may refer to you.

"Go confidently in the direction of your dreams. Live the life you have imagined."

— HENRY DAVID THOREAU

Chapter Eleven

Prepare to Prosper

At this point, your fear has been conquered, your skills sharpened, custom scripts tailored and your prospect list built and organized for maximum effectiveness. So now do you just pick up the phone and start dialling? No, not yet. This chapter addresses performance enhancing activities that will go a long way toward ensuring success.

Prepare Your Environment for Results

Whether making calls from your home or an office, it is important to prepare your surroundings to minimize any possible distractions. Here are a few suggestions.

- Seek Privacy: Most of us make calls from either our home or office. It is important to be undisturbed while making calls. Distractions will add frustration and waste time.

- Take Care of Incoming Calls: The time you dedicate to prospecting is for just that: *prospecting*. This means you should not take any incoming calls. You are in an important meeting (with yourself) that deserves the same respect as any other. You might want to forward your phone to another number that is either staffed or equipped with voice mail. Chances are good that you may call someone who cannot talk at that moment but may call you back before you have finished making your calls for the day. By having a secondary callback number or the call-forwarding option engaged, you will avoid interruption and avoid missing an important return call.

- Disable Call Waiting: I find the call waiting tone distracting while prospecting. To play it safe, I recommend disabling this feature while prospecting. You may find the instructions to disable call waiting in your local phone book, or just call your local phone company. They will be glad to help you.

- Cellular Phones: The portable nature of today's cellular phones makes them a popular choice for today's business professional. Today's cellular phones are a great business tool, especially when seeking privacy. However, nothing is worse than a bad connection. A weak cellular signal can spell disaster for prospecting calls. Therefore, for these important calls I suggest going landline wherever possible.

Additional Tips To Fortify Call Success

As we discussed in Chapter Three, setting the prospect at ease is the first important step in the successful phone contact. Relating to this are other factors that you can control to best influence the probability of your call being received as favorably as possible. Here are simple yet powerful suggestions that will have a strong impact on your calling success.

Prospect Empathy

Prospect Empathy is imagining what it is like to be on the receiving end of your call. What is happening in the prospects' environment? Are their surroundings comfortable or stressful? Here are a few things to keep in the forefront of your mind to help you develop prospect empathy.

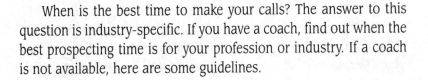

When is the best time to make your calls? The answer to this question is industry-specific. If you have a coach, find out when the best prospecting time is for your profession or industry. If a coach is not available, here are some guidelines.

When Calling A Private Residence

As a general rule, calls to a private residence become less popular with every minute after 9:15 p.m. or before 8:30 a.m. I suggest you set your schedule to <u>complete</u> your calls prior to 9:15 in the evening. The only exception is when you know for a fact that your prospect takes late-evening calls.

Similarly, calls around the dinner hour have their own issues. These can be handled quite well by opening with *"Did I catch you at a bad time?"* This technique allows you to assess the prospect's receptiveness to your call, as well as establish control of the conversation.

Practice Makes Permanent

Customized scripts have been proven to generate superior results. However, even the best script can fail if not delivered properly. To take full advantage of your work, it is a good idea to practice each script until your words sound confident and natural.

Practicing does not mean reading each script over once or twice. It means rehearsing first by yourself, then with a tape recorder, and finally with a coach. Solid hours of practice will pay dividends for years to come.

Practice Alone in Front of a Mirror

Find a quiet place and read your script as if you are speaking to a prospect. It is important that you hear your voice speaking your scripts. It also helps to <u>smile</u> when you read your scripts. It is true that a smile can be heard. Repeat each script until you begin to feel the words, inflections and pauses sounding natural.

Practice with a Tape Recorder

A simple tape recorder can be a powerful self-training tool. A tape recorder acts as a <u>voice mirror</u>, offering a true reflection of how you will sound to your prospect. Record your voice and play back each script, imagining that you are the receiver of the call. Do you sound confident, natural and in control? If not, practice until you do. Before you know it, you will.

Practice with a Coach

Ask a good friend or mentor to role play with you as you place calls to them. Ask the coach to assume the roles of Good Friend, Acquaintance and Referral. Ask for resistance in the form of some objections. Refer to your Appointment Pushback scripts to practice managing each response type. Ask your coach to give you honest feedback.

"There is one quality which one must possess to win, and that is definiteness of purpose, the knowledge of what one wants, and a burning desire to possess it."

— NAPOLEON HILL

Chapter Twelve

Beyond Goal Setting:
Getting Right Down To It

Now it is time to start making your calls. You may begin to feel some butterflies in your stomach as you sit with your list. Even after years of practice, it is common even for a skilled professional's heart to quicken and palms to sweat just before picking up the phone. A little discomfort is not necessarily a bad thing – especially if you are chasing a worthwhile dream or goal.

Goals: Essential to Success

Imagine you are an Olympic-class Archer. For years you've trained everyday with the hopes of representing your country at the Olympic Games. Over the years, you practiced and refined just how to stand, hold the bow, position the arrow, draw back, take aim and release. You are among the best archers on the planet.

It's the medal round of Olympic competition. You approach the line with quiet confidence only found in one who has stood there hundreds of times before. Armed with all the right equipment, backed up by the skill that only endless hours of practice can provide, you stand ready for the signal to start.

Just as the competition is about to commence, someone puts a blindfold over your eyes, spins you around a few times and says, *"Ok, now begin."* You cannot see the target! What do you think your chances are? There is no doubt that despite losing your ability to see, your training would enable you to properly hold and position the bow, find your arrow, place it on the string without hesitation, draw back on the bow and flawlessly release the arrow as you have done thousands of times before. However, without a target in sight, the chances of winning a medal, or for that matter hitting any target at all, are about zero. What a waste; a waste of time, a waste of talent and a waste of effort.

To get to the Olympic games, you had to make sure that you were equipped with the right tools and mentored by a knowledgeable coach. You invested countless hours of practice developing the right skills. All that time and effort invested, just to shoot an arrow blindly into the air?

Relate this archer's situation to the investment you have just made to improve and perfect your contacting and inviting skills. Your accomplishments to date are not trivial. If you have followed along, you are now armed with new tools, skills, attitude and knowledge. But all of these are useless without a well-defined, realistic and visible Goal for which to strive.

For 20 plus years, my earning and lifestyle have been completely dependent on my individual performance. One of the most critical lessons I learned is the importance of setting goals. A goal is a target that keeps you focused and on track. A properly defined goal is the foundation for the action plan that can give your days, weeks, months and even years, direction and clarity. The purpose of goal setting is to help understand where you are, and how far you must travel to reach your desired target. Once you know how far you must go, it is easy to figure out what activities will get you there.

For a goal to do its job, it must be visible to your mind's eye, believable (to you), well defined, and have a date. Once you know what you want and how much it will cost, putting the action plan in place is an essential component of your success formula. Let me share with you one of my personal goals and what I specifically need to do to predictably accomplish it this year.

I have always wanted a new Harley Davidson motorcycle. Not just any Harley Davidson motorcycle, but a vivid black Soft Tail Fat Boy. I made the decision to reward myself by paying cash for a new one this year. To make this happen, I must generate enough incremental income above what I earn today to cover the cash price of the motorcycle and a few minor (but necessary) accessories:
$20,000.

I am a visual person, meaning that to get excited about something, I need to actually see it. Knowing this about myself, I have sitting on my desk, on my refrigerator and on the sun visor of my car, a picture of my new vivid black Soft Tail Fat Boy. I see it at least four times a day, sometimes even more.

Now that I know what I want, when I want it and how much it will cost, I can put together an action plan to make it a reality. The process I used to make sure I reach this goal is best illustrated this way. I imagine myself standing at the edge of an open field of tall grass. In the middle of the field is my new vivid black, 667 pound chrome detailed Harley Davidson Fat Boy. I clearly see it in the distance. It comes to life with the sound of the engine calling: *here I am. You want me? Come get me!* There it is, my goal in plain sight. All I need to do is go out there and get it. I pause for a moment and stare as my pulse quickens. I close my eyes and imagine how great it will be to feel the wind rushing by as I roar down the road. But I suddenly realize that all the while I am dreaming of how great it will be that I'm standing still and not making one inch of progress. The clock is ticking. The longer I stare, the more time passes and the greater the risk of not reaching my goal.

So, I need to get moving. I need to take the necessary steps to walk out through the obstacles of distance and tall grass to claim my prize. All that is required now is an action plan. Then I must work the plan that will generate an incremental $20,000.00. My attitude echoes my commitment to reach this goal. Now, putting this plan in place is as easy as doing some simple math – backwards!

Simple Math – Done Backwards

Follow along with me as I go through my plan and the calculations needed to organize my goal into achievable activities. Before I can put together an action plan with the appropriate activity levels, I must have two critical pieces of information:

- My compensation plan (how money is earned)
- What activities generate results

Compensation:

By now you know that I am in professional sales. And, as such, I have a compensation plan that includes a quota and commission. Let's say for the sake of discussion that each incremental sale above my regular annual quota generates a net of $420. Knowing this, I simply divide the cash price of my goal by the net amount of an incremental sale: $420. (20,000 div.by 420 =47.6) We'll round up to 48 just to keep it simple. This means that my Harley Davidson Fat Boy can be defined as 48 incremental sales this year. Now all I need to do is put an action plan into place that will generate 48 additional sales.

Activities:

An action plan is made up of activities. In my business there are only 4 primary activities that generate sales.

They are:

- Prospecting Calls
- Face-to-Face Appointments
- Demonstrations
- Close

These are the only activities that generate money, and thus, are the activities I plan for and schedule before all others.

Backwards Math:

The next step is to work the numbers backwards to come up with the actual action plan of activities that will put my seat on the seat of my motorcycle. History has taught me that one out of two prospects who see a demonstration of my equipment become customers. Further, two out of four face-to-face appointments result in demonstrations, and four out of eight prospecting calls result in face-to-face appointments. So, 8 prospecting calls result in 4 face-to-face appointments that results in 2 demonstrations that will result in 1 sale. This means that all I need to do is contact and invite 8 additional prospects to explore doing business with my company and me per week to reach my goal. Simple, right? Well it gets even simpler.

I know that 8 incremental prospecting calls take about 15 minutes. That means my Harley Davidson is actually going to cost me about 15 additional minutes of contacting and inviting per week! *Rummmmmmmmmmmmm!* How easy is that? Can I find an additional 15 minutes per week to reach my goal? You bet I can – and I am! I use a simple form to do my backwards math. Take a look at the actual form used to set this particular goal.

Goal	Harley Davidson Fat Boy
Dollar Amount	$20,000
Incremental Sale Value	$420
# of Incremental Sales Required	48 per year (4 per month)

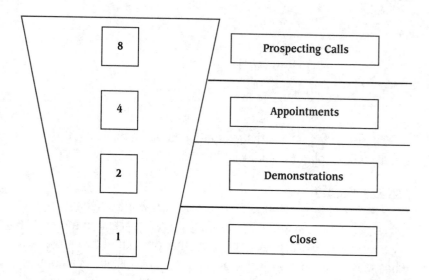

In principle, this formula can be used in most any business. You may want to seek the counsel of someone who is successful in your industry to make sure your assumptions and activities are in line with your goal.

In addition, I recommend keeping track of your efforts and results as you make progress towards your goal. I do this today the same way I have done it over the past 20 years. A simple timeline that tracks results to date, and what still needs to be accomplished, keeps my eye on the prize and assures that there are no surprises along the way. Keeping track of your progress this way will do two things for you. First, it makes it clear that time is always moving forward whether you are or not. Second, it will alert you early on if your results are not in line with your goal. If it appeared that I was falling behind, I would know about it in plenty of time to correct what wasn't working and get back on track. For example, if I look at my timeline in November and see that I have 39 sales to go, it is safe to say that I will miss my target. Look at the timeline below and you'll see what I mean.

	Jan	Feb	Mar	Apr	May	Jun	Jul	Aug	Sep	Oct	Nov	Dec
Monthly sales target	4	4	4	4	4	4	4	4	4	4	4	4
Actual Sales	6	4	3	4	7	9						
Sales To Go	42	38	35	31	24	15						

As you can see, I am actually outpacing my original plan – meaning I have enough momentum going to hit my goal of 48 sales early. As of the writing of this text, I have 15 more sales to go. Divide that by 4 targeted sales per month means I should be able to walk into my local Harley Davidson dealership and write a check for my Fat Boy a full two months ahead of schedule.

Does this mean I can relax a bit and perhaps slow down for a month or two? Not a chance. As I get closer to my goal, I look beyond to the next. I have learned through painful trial and error that to be successful and to maintain momentum, I must consistently set, plan and work for new goals. Sometimes goals are reached early, some on schedule and others need to be reset. The process is the same, but don't make the mistake of letting off the throttle as you near your goal. Make setting, working for and achieving goals a habit. I plan to set another major goal soon. Bigger than my Harley and one that will not only cause me to stretch, but is worth fighting for. I'll tell you all about it in the next book, but here's a hint: it flies!

Success Checklist:

Like a pilot who uses a checklist to insure that the jet taking his passengers across the Atlantic has all the required standards, you should follow this simple checklist to insure that your calls have the greatest impact.

✓ Set your first 8 appointments (with yourself)

Pick up your calendar and place a star (★) on the date 30 days from today. This is the day you will look back and see not only a marked improvement in both your contacting and inviting skills, but also an improvement in your business momentum. To insure this, you should schedule no less than your first 8 appointments with yourself. Two one-hour sessions per week will go a long way to getting your business momentum started. Dedicate these times to filling your calendar with productive business generating appointments – and nothing else. As each week passes, fill in two one-hour sessions four weeks out so that you are always placing productive business generating activities in front of all others.

As time goes on, and your skills improve, you may find that you can fill your calendar in only a one-hour session per week. Your calendar will tell you if you have too many appointments. Until then, I recommend no less than two one-hour sessions per week dedicated solely to contacting and inviting. Set these first eight appointments and be sure you keep them.

Note: If your current company or organization has recommended hours designated for prospecting which has proven successful, by all means follow those guidelines.

✓ Scripts:

Have the scripts you are going to use written out on a single side of paper.(Use the script builder forms located in the back of the book as a guideline.) Be sure to have a script for each prospect type; i.e. good friend, acquaintance, referral.

✓ Names list:

As stated earlier, your names list is the raw material of your business. Keep a paper copy of your updated names clearly illuminating those whom you have not yet called.

✓ **Quiet place:**

An appointment has three components: date, time and location. Your first eight appointments you schedule with yourself will require a private, quiet location to conduct business. Take care that there are no surprises relating to the location's availability and privacy.

✓ **Disable Call Waiting:**

If the phone you plan to use is equipped with that annoying distraction, the call waiting beep, be sure that you know how to disable it during your calling session. Most phone companies list the instructions at the front of the phone book. If not, a simple call to your phone company's customer service department will do the trick.

Set your First 8 Appointments	✓
Scripts	✓
Names List	✓
Private Location	✓
Disable Call Waiting	✓

In Chapter Two you were asked to write down some compelling reasons why your prospects would want to meet with you. Take a moment to review these reasons. Now ask yourself, do you believe them? Believing that you bring value to your prospects will help get the ball rolling.

For me, it is the value my company and equipment bring to my prospects, with value defined as:

- Better equipment reliability.
- Better print image quality.
- Faster service.

These advantages really make a positive difference to my customers. I am so convinced of these benefits that I am compelled to share them. Belief is a very powerful force, powerful enough to compel action. Belief in your product, your company and the service you provide makes it easier to speak confidently about how these advantages will benefit your prospects.

A little self-talk won't hurt either. Look at the first name on your prospect list and recite the following:

"{prospect's name} needs what I have to offer, knows I am looking out for them, and will be glad that I called".

Say this out loud a couple of times before you dial each phone number. Positive self-talk can fortify your resolve and make picking up the phone a breeze. Remember, you want to share something with a prospect that will enhance their lives. They need it, will be glad when they have it and will appreciate the fact that you thought of them. Like I said in Chapter Two, *"don't keep it a secret"*.

Always keep prospecting materials together in a file folder, a kind of <u>kit</u> where you keep everything necessary to make calls no matter where you are. This folder should contain your prospect list, a clean pad of paper and, of course, your custom scripts. Your <u>kit</u> could also contain some special photographs as positive motivators. These photographs should remind you what are working for and why you need to keep setting appointments. I have the latest pictures of my children, a house that I cannot yet afford and my latest goal, as well as one other very important photograph. Remember the first prospect call I made that almost ruined my career, the one where the receptionist ordered me out of the lobby in front of what seemed to be a thousand people? I took a picture of the front of that building and keep it in my folder.

Before starting my calls, I place these pictures on the desk or table in a very specific order: first my children's pictures, followed

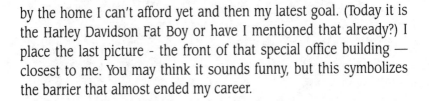

by the home I can't afford yet and then my latest goal. (Today it is the Harley Davidson Fat Boy or have I mentioned that already?) I place the last picture - the front of that special office building — closest to me. You may think it sounds funny, but this symbolizes the barrier that almost ended my career.

It is essential that you believe in what you are calling about. However, belief alone may not be enough to get you moving. I believed strongly that I represented a great company with superior products and excellent service before and after walking into that building. However, it is clear that belief alone is not enough to keep going. I need constant reminders of what motivates me. Looking at the picture of the office building keeps fresh in my mind how silly it would be to let one <u>rude</u> person hold me back.

Do you have a strong, compelling reason to stay focused? Is it your family, your children, a certain goal that you have always dreamed about? Great — get some pictures that represent what you want, what is important and what you will fight for. Keeping your eye on the prize is not just some cute saying; it is true, powerful and necessary for long-term success. Place these pictures in a folder and carry them with you at all times. Oh, one more thing. Get a small piece of cheesecloth and put that in with the pictures as well. Just before you make your calls, take out your prospecting kit and arrange these pictures on the desk or table in front of you. Now place the piece of cheesecloth in front of all that is important. The cheesecloth stopped one of the most powerful predators dead in it's tracks. To you, it represents fear, hesitation and procrastination. Don't let *"cheesecloth"* keep you from what you really want and what is truly important to you. Armed with new knowledge, attitude and skill, it looks kind of silly there, doesn't it? Do you think it can hold you back? I didn't think so, either.

"All our dreams can come true if we have the courage to pursue them"

— WALT DISNEY

Summary

Look at all that you have already accomplished. Over the past pages you have:

1. Discovered a new way of thinking, an empowering perspective on setting appointments. And, you are now in control of False Enemy Appearing Real (or phone FEAR).

2. Mastered the skill of custom script building using STEER™ You have proven to yourself that you <u>can</u> effectively use the phone to set appointments with qualified prospects.

3. Learned a prospect list development strategy that, when executed properly, will keep you waist deep in quality names for as long as your dreams drive you down the road of achievement and success.

4. Prepared yourself and your environment for maximum performance, success and effectiveness.

Get It in Gear!
All the ability, skill and enthusiasm are for naught without action. The fastest vehicle stands still in neutral even if the motor is running. Now is the time to put your machine in gear.

Dream vs. Fantasy
Having a crystallized dream is vital. You must have compelling internal motivation to go the extra mile, endure the uncomfortable and have the staying power to win. Therefore, a word of caution:

115

don't let your dreams turn into fantasies. Dreams without action quickly become mere fantasies.

It feels great to imagine how wonderful it will be when you can afford that new house, boat or Harley-Davidson, or to be debt-free. But remember that just thinking about it does not get the job done. You must put your new skills to work in order to make progress.

I am not saying you should not keep your dreams in front of you. Writing them down, posting pictures on the refrigerator or even paying a visit to the local Mercedes-Benz dealership can help keep you focused. I am saying you should get moving and consistently do the productive activities that propel business forward. At this point, action is all that remains.

In any business there are four productive activities that will ensure success.

1. Setting appointments.
2. Presenting products and services.
3. Securing customer commitment.
4. Coaching others.

That is it. Other activities may be important, but make no mistake — do not confuse them with the real work that moves you closer to your goals. The above activities must be daily business priorities at the top of your workday schedule.

The first three activities need no explanation by now. Without setting a calendar full of appointments, your performance will suffer. Presenting your product or service is the purpose of your appointments. Gaining customer commitment turns a prospect into a happy new customer/associate and keeps the financial engine running.

The fourth activity, coaching others, is also critical to success. It is no secret that depending on one's own efforts alone limits potential. Leveraging the effort and momentum of others builds their success while securing your own. Imagine for a moment that your contacting fears have been put to rest, your skills are sharp and your calendar is full of appointments with people who want to see you. You're on a roll and your goals are in sight.

I can only think of one thing that would surpass that feeling: knowing I have helped an entire team or, better yet, an army of people like me to defeat their contacting fears; develop sharp skills; and fill their calendars with appointments. It is a great feeling not only to benefit from the efforts of others, but also to touch the lives of people in a positive way by helping them move closer to their own dreams.

What are the primary activities that will move your business forward? Turn to the last page of the book and write them down. You might want to tear this page out and keep it with you. Periodically stop what you are doing and look at the activity list you just made. Are you doing one of those activities now? If not, think about what you are doing, what you really want, and consider the other people that need your help. Then get moving. The clock is ticking.

Good Friends	
Name	Phone Number

Name	Aquaintance Phone Number	How Will They Remember You?

Name	Phone Number	Who Referred You?	How Do They Know The Referring Party?

Custom Script Builder
Good Friend

Set at Ease

> Statement of
> Familiarity

_____

_____

_____

Take Control

> Confirm Prospect is
> open to talk

_____

_____

_____

Ethusiastically Assume Appointment

> Increase Interest –
> decrease time
> commitment

_____

_____

_____

_____

_____

Expect then Manage Pushback

Reaffirm after Confirming

> Write it in Stone

_____

_____

_____

_____

Expect then Manage Pushback
Good Friend

Status Quo

> No Need!
> I am already happy!

No Time

> I don't have time
> to look!

Brush Off

> Send me some info.
> I'll get back to you.

Tell Me More

> Tell me all the
> details Now!

Custom Script Builder
Acquaintance

Set at Ease

Statement of Familiarity

Take Control

Confirm Prospect is open to talk

Ethusiastically Assume Appointment

Increase Interest – decrease time commitment

Expect then Manage Pushback

Reaffirm after Confirming

Write it in Stone

Expect then Manage Pushback

Acquaintance

Status Quo

No Need!
I am already happy!

No Time

I don't have time
to look!

Brush Off

Send me some info.
I'll get back to you.

Tell Me More

Tell me all the
details Now!

Custom Script Builder
Referral

Set at Ease

> Statement of Familiarity

Take Control

> Confirm Prospect is open to talk

Ethusiastically Assume Appointment

> Increase Interest – decrease time commitment

Expect then Manage Pushback

Reaffirm after Confirming

> Write it in Stone

Expect then Manage Pushback
Referral

Status Quo

No Need!
I do business with
someone else

No Time

I don't have time
to look!

Brush Off

Send me some info.
I'll get back to you.

Tell Me More

Tell me all the
details Now!

Primary activities to Move My Business Forward

About the Author:

Upon graduation from the Rochester Institute of Technology in 1983, Ron Baker began his career with Eastman Kodak. Earning top sales honors, he progressed to Marketing Education Specialist, Sales Manager and Worldwide Product Line Manager.

Ron continues his sales career at Xerox Corporation and today consistently turns in over-quota performance as a Production Systems specialist in upstate New York.

He is also co-founder of Sales Boot Camp, Inc., a consulting and sales training firm that develops and delivers customized skill-building programs designed to increase the effectiveness, profit potential and longevity of entrepreneurs and marketing professionals.

To invite Ron Baker to inspire and empower your organization, visit him at www.contactingandinvitingmadeeasy.com or by calling Sales Boot-Camp Inc. at 1-800-835-9044.